May you see yourself with clear,
kind, and loving eyes.
May you move through the world
with ease, grace, and strength.

MODERN GUIDE

to

ENERGY CLEARING

About the Author

Barbara Moore is an author, teacher, and student of wonder and magic, particularly of the unseen energies that course through all that is. Decades before she discovered magical paths and practices, Barbara experimented with magic and working with energy. At the same time, her studies in tarot and shamanism expanded, shaped, and solidified her ideas about energy work. These explorations led to a way of understanding and flowing through the world based on practical experience.

Get to know Barbara via her website: www.tarotshaman.com.

for my sister
Michelle Palazzolo
because she asked for it

CONTENTS

INTRODUCTION 1

Part 1: Spiritual and Energetic Well-Being 9

Chapter 1: Defining Terms 13

Chapter 2: Energy Health Basics 23

Part 2: Personal Care 31

Chapter 3: Energy-Clearing Techniques 37

Chapter 4: Techniques for Containing and
Cultivating Energy 63

Chapter 5: Preparing to Clear 93

Chapter 6: Identifying Emotional Blocks 103

Chapter 7: Identifying Mental Misdirection 119

Chapter 8: Your Personal Energy Practice 139

Part 3: Your Environment 155

Chapter 9: Your Personal Space 157

Chapter 10: Co-Creating the World
Through Blessings 179

CONCLUSION 197

APPENDIX A: A SAMPLING OF BLESSINGS 199

APPENDIX B: SERVING THE OLD BONE MOTHER 203

BIBLIOGRAPHY 207

INDEX 211

INTRODUCTION

When my publisher asked me to write a book on energy clearing, my initial reaction was "But that's not my area of expertise; I don't know nearly enough to fill a book." Initial reactions can be tricky. Sometimes they are inspired moments of knowing (also called intuition). Most times, though, they are reactions shaped by deeply furrowed patterns that may or may not be based in truth. After releasing the initial fear about taking on a new challenge, I was able to respond more thoughtfully.

As it turns out, I've consciously worked with energy for most of my adult life, even before I was grounded in a wide understanding of a variety of New Age ideas. While these stories I'm about to share may not have been my first attempts at deliberate energy working, they are the first I remember. Without any experience in or knowledge of modern magic, I created a ritual to help my sister sell her home and one to help a friend's husband find a job. They worked. Both were simple rituals, designed in ways that made sense to me and that used things found in most middle-class suburban homes. My understanding and practice grew slowly at first and then more quickly when I discovered New Age materials. The culmination of my current understanding came together only a few months before being asked to write this book.

In April 2016 I was a main-stage presenter at the annual tarot conference in New York called Readers Studio. Tarot is my recognized area of expertise. Since the late 1980s I've written many books, designed decks, given readings, presented at conferences all over the world, and taught students in person and online through a year-long correspondence course.

To me, tarot is far more than a divination tool. It is a sacred text that contains something more important than ways to peek into the future. Within the cards I find spiritual wisdom and practical teachings. Tarot has become the lens through which I see the world. How does tarot apply to energy work? There is a direct connection. Don't worry, though; after this story, tarot won't be mentioned again.

Most people who want to learn the cards focus almost entirely on the card meanings, which, of course, are important. But many people get frustrated when they try to do a reading. Readings that focus only on the card meanings are often disjointed at best and confusing at worst. You see, in the space between cards is where the real magic occurs. All the cards have a specific energy. When we simply observe the energy of the card in isolation, nothing much happens. When the cards interact is when they come to life. When the cards are read in relation to each other, it is easier to see what is actually happening in a situation.

After assessing the situation, we can use the cards to determine advice. We do this by bringing in other cards that represent actions the seeker can take. We analyze the probable results. If the results are not what the seeker prefers, we try other cards. We figure out what kind of energy to tap in to in order to create the desired (or best possible) result. Years of paying attention to how the energy of the cards affects each other enhanced my understanding of working with energy in my daily life. But this is not what my 2016 presentation was about.

Ironically, my two-and-a-half-hour workshop did not focus on how to read the cards or sharing a new technique. Instead, it was about clearing our space, both internally and externally, in order to be better people and thereby better readers. It is kind of funny how this thinking has become such a part of the way I look at and move through the world that I didn't even realize that I do, in fact, have an understanding of and experience in energy work.

WHAT TO EXPECT

My understanding evolved slowly and through everyday experiences. I didn't learn some complex esoteric system or take training through a trademarked or certified energy school or teacher. There is nothing wrong with those paths if they are your paths and if they resonate with the deep chord of your heart. But if you are reading this book, I suspect you are like me and favor personal experience and intimate connections that spring from within rather than taking on the cloak of someone else's practice.

This book is for you if you are looking for a clear way of understanding energy, seeking practices that help you to live more freely, and hoping to improve yourself, your environment, and even the larger world around you. This is, in fact, the main goal of becoming adept at energy management: to be unencumbered of anything that takes away your free will and causes you to act in ways that are not in accordance with your ideals.

The ideas presented here will be written in as neutral a language as possible, broad enough to be adaptable to your personal beliefs because—and this is *very important*—I'm not promoting a specific practice complete in itself with specific lists of what you must do. Instead, I offer you general ideas, concepts, and practices that can be mixed and matched and modified so that they reflect your truth. The wisest teachers don't ask you to accept their wisdom but rather lead you to the threshold of your own wisdom. I don't necessarily claim to be wise, but I do believe a good teacher guides and encourages rather than dictates. I offer these ideas based on my personal experience and understanding freely, with no expectation other than to inspire you. If I can find my way to a personal understanding and set of useful and effective practices, so can you. In fact, I am still finding my way. Every single day, as I learn and experience more, my ideas and practices change, and I hope yours do, too.

My understanding of energy and magic was the result of just living my life in the best way I knew how. Energy work is a kind of magic, the kind of magic that creates change in the world according to your will. A long time ago I heard this story about magic that really rang true for me; it applies just as well to energy work. Here is the story as I remember it:

> There was a farmer who sought out the advice and magic of the local wise woman. He wanted to learn how his farm could be more prosperous. She gave him a bag of sand and told him to walk around the perimeter of his property every morning for a year and a day, dropping a grain of sand every few feet. Over the first few weeks he noticed things like sections of the fence needing repair, damage to the edges of certain crops, and evidence of intrusive weeds. He began carrying some basic tools and materials on his walks, taking care of things as he found them. He was able to closely observe where things grew well and where they didn't. He cleared debris after storms and planted trees as wind breaks in exposed areas. As the year progressed, he diligently dropped the grains of sand and attended to his land. The next year his property was in good repair, his crops abundant, and his animals healthy.

Were those magical grains of sand? Maybe; maybe not. Perhaps the real magic was the attention paid to what was going on around him.

What does this have to do with energy clearing? We usually look for ways to clear energy when we feel that something is wrong, just as we often only go to the doctor when we don't feel well. There are definitely ways to correct, cleanse, or clear energy that is inappropriate, stagnant, or just not right. Some may call it negative energy, but that duality doesn't make sense to me because all energy comes from the Divine. Furthermore, labeling energy as "positive" or "negative" makes us lazy in our observations and identification of energy. Instead, if we talk of "inappropriate" energy, we are encouraged to identify in what ways it is inappropriate and what would be more appropriate or desirable. The more specific we are, the more effective our work can be.

In addition to paying attention to understanding the nature of energy, I talk both about energy clearing and energy cultivation because the two go hand in hand. After you've cleared out the energy that you don't want, it makes sense to bring in (and cultivate) the energy that you *do* want. Once any immediate issues are dealt with, we can create healthy spaces within ourselves and our environment. Through good energetic health practices, we create spaces that are resistant to inappropriate energy and are easy to maintain. Just like we don't brush our teeth once and consider it done for life, our spiritual energy thrives best with consistent habits that support health and vitality. This is true of our personal energy and of the energy in our surroundings.

When we take care of our own energy, we are more stable and able to attend to the energy around us. After clearing and containing basic health, we can cultivate the energy within us and around us to support certain qualities or goals such as protection, abundance, kindness, or creativity. We attend to ourselves so that we are stronger, liberated, and able to live our soul's purpose in the world. In short, we attend to our own energy so that we can create ourselves and become the people we want to be. And if the people we want to be are people who want to heal and care for the world we live in and those who share it with us, so much the better.

YOUR PRACTICE, NOT MY SYSTEM

The approach to energetic health that I suggest is *not* a step-by-step system but rather a template or recipe. People are such unique beings and situations are so complex that it is unrealistic to think that any one approach will be right for everyone or even a majority of people. It is also unrealistic to think that doing the exact same things every day will suffice since each day brings new energy and new challenges. A more flexible, customized approach increases the probability of success. Not only are you more likely to do a practice that fits into your life, the focus will be more specific to your needs, which can change daily.

You will notice that the thinkers who have most influenced my ideas about energy work come from a broad range of subjects as well as various spiritual paths. So much wisdom can easily cross categories. A few decades ago, when I was learning to knit, the incomparable Elizabeth Zimmerman shaped my approach. A prolific author and highly respected teacher, Zimmerman rarely provided normal patterns detailing precisely how many or what kind of stitches to make. Instead, she taught general principles and provided examples of how to use that information to create precisely what you wanted. She empowered knitters to experiment and, above all, to trust themselves, saying, "I deliberately keep my knitting notes vague, because tastes vary, and your brains are as good as mine anyway."[1] This is true. Your brains *are* as good as mine. I may have read more about this topic, practiced longer,

---

1   Elizabeth Zimmerman, *The Opinionated Knitter* (Pittsville, WI: Schoolhouse Press, 2005), 31.

and spent more time exploring the general principles of energetic health, but in this book I'm sharing all I know. Once you've read it, the only thing you don't have, perhaps, is experience. Using your perfectly lovely brains, common sense, and knowledge of yourself and your life, you can incorporate these principles to achieve your own goals. Based on my own experiences and the information in these pages, I share ideas and suggestions to get you started on your path to becoming the free and awesome person you were born to be.

Energy clearing and cultivation are neither hard nor complicated. You don't have to subscribe to any specific tradition, belief system, or religion. Part 1 will establish a foundational understanding. This includes using clear, common language to create a shared vocabulary that will make it easier to talk about the nature of energy. We will also discuss in greater detail the purpose of energy work. The language and purpose will help us have realistic expectations about what we are going to do and how we are going to do it.

The most important work will be your own personal clearing, which is covered in part 2. Personal clearing includes creating a toolkit of techniques that you can use in different circumstances as needed, clearing long-standing energy blocks within yourself and developing an energetic maintenance practice. You can try the techniques as presented and keep notes in a journal about how they worked for you, as well as ideas for modifying the techniques to better suit you. After you've tried some techniques for yourself, you will use a simple step-by-step process to help you develop a practice that works for you and the life you are living right now. There will be no need to completely overhaul your life or purchase any special items. These ideas can slip easily into your already existing day, as naturally as washing your face or putting on your shoes.

Part 3 moves beyond ourselves and into the greater world. After you are feeling cleared and centered, we move outward, learning about the energy of spaces and places and how you can affect the energy of your home, workplace, car, etc. Finally, you'll learn how simple practices can change the world, one small action at a time.

As mentioned earlier, this book is a guide, not a manifesto of dogma. You will get the most out of it if you read it with a journal (and, of course, a writing utensil) alongside. There will be exercises for you to try and suggestions for lists, reflections, and general journal entries. Together, your journal and this book will help you create your own personal energy practice.

PART 1

SPIRITUAL AND ENERGETIC WELL-BEING

Energy clearing and cultivation are great practices for making your home, office, or even your car feel good and safe. You can use these ideas to help support your own physical, mental, and emotional well-being. Good energy management can create a life with greater balance and peace, but energy work goes much further than that. In fact, consistent energy clearing and cultivation is essential to living your soul's purpose, and that's pretty exciting.

The idea of your soul's purpose is a powerful but often misunderstood phrase. Too often we think that our soul's purpose is like a glorified career guidance counselor that will tell you what to do to earn a living, as if our soul came to this earth to gain a specific job title. It makes sense that we think that because our culture really drives home the point that we are what we do for a living. The truth is that our job title can be *part* of how we express our soul's purpose. Our soul's purpose is the reason and the way we do what we do rather than *what* we do. To complicate things further, your soul's purpose isn't just one word or sentence. It isn't something finite but rather an ongoing dance between you and the Divine. With each step of the dance we are changed, so our soul's purpose—or at least our conscious understanding of it—evolves. The more we live it, the more it reveals itself to us. Perhaps the simplest way I can describe it is that your soul's purpose is the collection of ideals that you hold most dear—the ideals that you are willing to do whatever it takes to live up to.

But who among us fully lives up to our own ideals each and every minute of every day? I know I don't. This means that our soul's purpose is something we express in the world, and it is also our North Star that guides us through the dark, confusing times as well as affirms our steps during easier, clearer times. I heard an interesting tidbit: airplanes are off-course 90 percent of the time. Pilots are always course-correcting and learn that they have to continually adjust for changing circumstances.[2] Sometimes I feel like my life is like that, that I'm kind of heading in the right direction but also kind of not. During those times, I find it's important to pay attention to my energy and the energy around me in order to correct my course. That is another benefit of good energy health. The more robust your energetic health, the easier it is to tell when you are offtrack.

Thinking about energy work, living your soul's purpose, and just plain old living life as a continuous sequence of course corrections is actually a relief. Knowing that the point is the journey and that we are not required or even meant to ever completely "arrive" takes the pressure off. We are allowed and expected to make mistakes. Mistakes are valuable teaching moments especially with energy work. We cannot quantify and measure and label this work in any sort of scientific manner, so we really do have to rely on our experience. Because of that, energy work does not require a complete lifestyle change.

In fact, overhauling your life would be more of an effective distraction from the real work of developing sustainable practice in your life right now. For example, minimalism is very popular right

---

2   *Airplane Flying Handbook FAA-H80833B* (Oklahoma City, OK: US Department of Transportation, 2016), 6–2.

now and while it does draw from ideas about energy work, some of the minimalist techniques are just too overwhelming for most of us to adopt easily. I rarely have time to clean a drawer or closet; it's unlikely my family and I would have the time for a packing party. A packing party is where you invite people over to help you pack up your house, even everyday essentials, as if you are moving in one day. Then you unpack what you need as you need it. After three weeks, whatever isn't unpacked gets thrown away, donated, or sold. For some this is the perfect approach, but it can make others feel defeated before they begin. Instead, the energy clearing and cultivation that I practice simply involves one good decision at a time within the life you are currently living.

In order to make good decisions, to make appropriate course corrections, and to live your soul's purpose, you have to be energetically clear. Think about your ideals. In fact, write them down. What beliefs mean the most to you? When you are between a rock and a hard place, what ideal helps you decide what to do? What matters to you? Those things are the essence of your soul's purpose. Once you have your list, think about your past twenty-four hours. In what ways did your behavior, actions, words, feelings, and thoughts reflect your cherished ideals? Which ones did not? If you are like me, some things really are expressions of your values and some are not.

Joshua Fields Millburn (one of the Minimalists) often says in his podcasts that if you show him your budget and your schedule, he can name your values.[3] He means this in a slightly provocative way because, for most of us, our budgets and schedules do not reflect our true values but rather what we *think* we are supposed to value. It is a statement meant to make us think seriously about

3   Joshua Fields Millburn, *Minimalist Podcast*, http://www.theminimalists .com/podcast/.

how we spend our time and our money. If we are human beings with free will and the ability to make conscious decisions, why do we make decisions about our time, money, and behavior that separate us from our values rather than embody them? That is a great question. In fact, it might be *the* question: "Why do I behave in ways that are not in alignment with my beliefs and ideals?"

One answer is "Well, I am only human." That works, but it is also a cop-out. No one really likes to think about where they've fallen short, unless they like to beat themselves up about it for a while. Yet these moments—these mistakes or failures—are road signs that point us to where we can find energy issues that need attention. In order to live our soul's purpose, in order to live our values in our daily lives, we need to be free from energetic disharmony; to do this, identify the points of departure from our guiding values, figure out what caused the discrepancy, and deal with it. Then we can more easily correct our course toward becoming the people we truly want to be. The alternative is to be controlled, reacting to life rather than engaging with it in a mindful and meaningful way.

The next two chapters lay the foundation for our exploration of energy clearing. First we will establish a shared vocabulary. After that, we will discuss the basics of energetic health.

Spiritual and energetic health and well-being is about so much more than waving around a burning stick of sage or plugging in a salt lamp (although those things are really useful). It is about knowing what you value and keeping yourself free so that you can live those values in your own beautiful and unique way. You have great medicine in you that the world desperately needs. So pick up that sage bundle and let's get to work so that you can express your glorious soul, support other glorious souls, and heal our world.

CHAPTER 1

DEFINING TERMS

As we begin our journey into the world of energy clearing and cultivation, it will be helpful to have a basic understanding of main terms that will come up throughout the discussion of spiritual and energetic well-being. Here we'll get into the meanings of energy, vibration, movement, and more. But before we delve into those specifics, we will first take a step back and look at the larger picture. Approaching a subject that is hard to nail down and define with any sort of quantifiable certainty is best served with a broad view.

Joseph Campbell studied myths from different cultures and different times. He noticed repeating patterns of characters and plots that differed in particulars but shared many common qualities across the miles and across the ages. It was like the creative outpourings of the human soul were all experiencing and seeking similar milestones. Likewise, most of us are familiar with the idea of archetypes: collectively shared unconscious ideas, images, and patterns of thoughts that have the same root but can be expressed with individualized details. Focusing on the specific and differing details rather than the shared big picture, whether in myth or religion, archetypal images, or symbols, is better for causing division and arguments than facilitating understanding. Looking at the shared larger patterns allows for a more inclusive attitude, which makes discussion easier because instead of arguing over semantics, we can focus on areas of agreement.

Talking about metaphysical energy can be really challenging because we lack ways to accurately measure, separate, and identify metaphysical energy and often rely on belief and personal experience to shape our understanding. The broad population of people interested in energy work includes many different spiritual, religious, and intellectual traditions (or combinations thereof) or even the complete lack of any sort of path. Because each person, path, or tradition has their own vocabulary for understanding and discussing energy, like Joseph Campbell and his megamyths and Carl Jung and his archetypes, we will search underneath the various words to find shared understanding.

The information and ideas presented here are not based on any one tradition or practice. However, it would quickly become cumbersome to use even a partially inclusive list of specific words every time we mention a concept. So, for ease of writing (and reading!), we will use a vocabulary that is broad, understandable, acceptable, and (I sincerely hope) inoffensive. If you have a different word that means the same thing, simply substitute that word in your mind as you are reading.

We will cover five terms. The explanations of the words are longer than usual glossary entries because it is important to be clear from the start. First we will define what we mean by *energy*. The terms *vibration* and *movement* will explore two characteristics of energy. Energy exists everywhere, but to begin we need to focus on ourselves, so we will take a quick overview of the basic components of our *energy body*. Finally, we will discuss the goal of energy work: *energetic harmony*.

ENERGY

In this book we are exploring metaphysical energy, sometimes identified by words like chi, prana, spirit, or essence. Some energy in our physical world is either visible or measurable through scientific means, but this is not the type of energy we mean when we talk about metaphysical energy. Metaphysical energy is the energy that we cannot see or measure or identify through Western scientific means. This doesn't mean it is not real. Our experience tells us that it is indeed real.

Most of us have walked into rooms or met people and immediately sensed that either something is attractive and pleasant or something is off-putting or worse. We may talk about a place having a bad vibe or a person having good mojo. We may find a certain person's presence calming or a certain place or circumstance jarring. If you've had any of those kinds of experiences, then you are aware of metaphysical energy. Perhaps you only notice it if it is extreme, and that's a totally normal response. Through practice, experience, and intention, you can build your skills in identifying and managing energy.

Even though we sometimes say that something has negative energy or a bad vibe, energy is not good or bad, positive or negative. It can be inappropriate or stagnant, which can *feel* bad or negative. This is an important point because thinking that bad vibes are everywhere or that we could fall victim to negative energy creates an environment of fear. Fear leads us to close down, creating stagnation, or to lash out, creating an inappropriate use of energy, both of which continue an unhealthy cycle.

Our culture perpetuates this belief, so when we encounter inappropriate or stagnant energy we try to separate ourselves from it or destroy it. Neither of these methods works in the long term, even though they may give some temporary relief or sense of safety. We cannot separate ourselves from what we might think of as negative energy because everything that exists is really all connected and we are all one. By understanding energy clearing and cultivation, we learn to transform energy that has become stagnant or inappropriate.

Labeling energy as negative has another downside. It is mental judgment, and—like most mental judgment (which differs from discernment)—it is lazy. The opposite of mental judgment is mental curiosity. When we are curious about something, such as "negative" energy, we are invited to look more deeply at the situation. We learn to assess, identify, and understand what is going on so that we can take productive steps to re-establish harmony rather than lashing out or shutting down.

Whether we consciously work with energy or not, it flows into and out of us. If we do not attend to it, then currents of energy buffet us around and we spend our time reacting to it. It is like people who aren't very disciplined about time management and are always in a "putting out fires" mode. They can still be productive but they are often stressed and perhaps not able to do their best work. When we work with energy deliberately, we have more control not only of ourselves but also of the energy we allow to flow back into the world. We can take in energy that is stagnant or inappropriate and ground it back into the earth, where it can be cleared or redistributed to a more appropriate situation, or we can transform it within ourselves and release it into our lives and the world.

VIBRATION

When we say something or someone has a bad vibe, that is shorthand for a bad vibration. So, again, our experience tells us that energy has a vibration. When an energy's vibration is off due to stagnation, we say it is bad. An energy's vibration may be off, but that doesn't mean the energy is bad; it means that the energy has to be managed. Through our actions or even our thoughts, we can change an energy's vibration, bringing it back into harmony.

Energy may be meant to vibrate at a lower or higher frequency than it is. Lower vibrations aren't always bad and, in fact, are connected with the deepest, most grounding earth energies, which can sometimes be the most appropriate energy for the situation. Higher vibrations aren't always good. Vibrations that are too high for the situation can create anxiety and stress. Being a good energy manager takes a subtle and nuanced understanding; things are not always black and white.

MOVEMENT

One of the easiest types of energy to identify is stagnant energy, probably because it is so prevalent and also because it is so uncomfortable. Energy is meant to flow. However, we are taught to think in terms of acquiring, gathering, hoarding, and saving physical resources (such as money, food, and possessions). Even though this applies to our physical experience, it becomes part of our energetic understanding.

There is a tenet in some traditions called the principle of correspondence, often expressed in the phrase "as above, so below; as below, so above." This means that when something happens on one plane of existence, it happens on another. For example, an emotional trauma (the emotional plane) can cause illness (the physical plane). When we practice acquiring and hoarding in the physical world, we cultivate that same energy in our energy body and thereby create and attract that kind of stagnant energy.

The cool thing is that setting stagnant energy free is easy and often really fun and satisfying, except in the most extreme circumstances. Once you get used to living in a state of flowing energy, you will not want to live in a state of stagnation ever again.

Good energetic health isn't black and white, though. While flowing energy is healthy energy, that doesn't mean chaotic, uncontrolled, scattered energy is better. If we do not have a good sense of our own center and a strong, grounded connection to that center, we are blown about by any other energy that comes our way. We are reactive rather than responsive.

While our culture has cultivated the ideal of stagnation through acquisition, it has also cultivated in us a tendency toward ungroundedness. As unpopular as this idea might sound, the technology that has made our lives better in so many ways (who doesn't love having their whole music or audio book collection in their pocket?) has also eaten away at our sense of groundedness, focus, and intent. Every time our phones vibrate or bling or sing, our attention is pulled away from our center. We are urged to react rather than respond, and this state of being eats away at our free will.

ENERGY BODY

We all have physical bodies and (hopefully) an understanding of what our body is, how it works, and how to take care of it. We also all have energy bodies, sometimes called auric, subtle, or etheric bodies. Some traditions identify different layers of the energy body and have sophisticated diagrams of how they work. As you develop your own understanding, you may wish to explore some of these more nuanced systems.

The ideas in this book will give you a good foundation to build on if you wish to pursue more intricate systems. However, it is not necessary to use complex energy body systems in order to create and maintain a healthy energy body. We can take a simpler approach that is fine in itself or as a springboard to other methods. Many models have the energy body and the physical body separate, with the energy body existing a few inches or a few feet from the physical body. While I think we can feel our energy beyond our physical body, I do not separate the energetic body (or, indeed, the spiritual body) from the physical body. Whether your personal model separates them or not should not affect the usefulness of the concepts here.

We will focus on some of the most basic aspects of energy— the most easily recognizable and the most commonly recognized parts: mental and emotional as well as the boundary area, which is like your energy body's skin. Even though we will explore these different parts, it is important to not get too bogged down in what part is called what and what each part does. We love to separate and to name things because when we know something's name, we feel we have some control over it or at least an understanding of it.

Our culture is fond of naming, categorizing, and compartmentalizing things, which is definitely a useful practice for certain ways of understanding the world. One downside is that this approach perpetuates the myth of separation. This myth (some refer to it as the "lie of separation") tells us we are separate from everything else that exists—that we are separate from each other and that the various parts of ourselves are separate from each other.

When we think in terms of our mind or our heart, we may be tempted to overvalue one and denigrate the other. Culturally, the tendency is to overvalue logic and denigrate intuition. For those of us who have left mainstream culture to pursue other ways of understanding the world, it is natural to swing in the other direction and overvalue intuition over rationality. Both of these approaches put a vital aspect of our humanity in shadow, and whenever anything is in shadow, it expresses itself however it can, often with destructive results.

One timely example is the 2016 Oxford Dictionaries Word of the Year: post-truth. Post-truth describes a culture where political debate focuses on emotional reactions rather than policy and facts. As we know, for several hundred years our culture has denigrated the emotional and intuitive side of human understanding in favor of the rational approach. This places the intuitive and emotional aspects of human nature collectively into shadow. Anything that is forced into shadow becomes twisted, bitter, and resentful, as would anything or anyone that is shoved in a dark place and called bad names. So while considering issues from an intuitive or emotional viewpoint isn't necessarily bad, it becomes very problematic when our collective emotional life has transformed into something twisted. Our current post-truth society is reacting from wounded emotions rather than healthy ones … and it shows, no matter which side of the divide you are on. It is important to understand how all the parts work in relation to each other so that the whole self can be stronger and healthier, with nothing hidden in shadow waiting to blow up in our faces.

Our energy bodies are like our physical bodies in that they have a boundary. Like skin, our physical body's boundary, the boundary of our energy body is permeable. We can control the extent of this permeability so that we only take in the energy we want. In addition, our energy body is sticky; it is easy for energy to cling to us. Understanding energy management helps us to be aware of all types of energy around us so that we are not infiltrated or polluted by energy that isn't beneficial to our balance and harmony.

ENERGETIC HARMONY

Energetic harmony is the goal of energy clearing and cultivation. Some people (myself included) think of it as being grounded and centered. However, *energetic harmony* is a more precise phrase because it has a greater sense of appropriateness and flexibility than does *grounded and centered*, which is really only one aspect of energetic harmony. Harmony inspires ideas about a wide range of possibilities, any of which might be appropriate depending on circumstances. A full understanding of being grounded and centered also includes that same sense of appropriateness. However, for many people there is a connotation of heaviness with being grounded.

Another phrase that people use for energetic harmony is balance. In its truest sense, balance is also a great word for this concept. However, as with being grounded and centered, the common meaning misses the mark. Many people think that balance means simply combining equal parts of things, such as making sure your life has equal amounts of work and leisure. Such strict equations don't apply to nature or to human life. In nature there are seasons for different activities. In our lives it is necessary sometimes to work more than to rest, such as preparing for a large event or studying for final exams. At other times, such as while recovering from an illness or grieving a loss, we need to rest more rather than work. Understanding healthy balance improves with experience and by paying attention.

Energetic harmony is not a static state but is in constant flux, adjusting as needed to account for changes in surrounding energy, intent, or need. The difference between reacting and responding is one of the most important things to understand, and we will come back to this idea again and again. Being in a state of energetic harmony means that we are able to *respond* to the world around us, to our interior needs, and to other people or circumstances in a calm, thoughtful way. We are able to reflect and make conscious choices. The flip side of this is *reacting* to the world, to every thought and emotion that passes through us, or to the actions and words of others. Reacting is a way of behaving that is similar to a knee-jerk reaction. Something happens and we have an instant reaction. We are controlled rather than truly choosing.

These days people talk a lot about triggers. Triggers are reactions, not responses. We had an experience. We suffered a trauma. Now we have an embedded reaction to certain situations. This means we no longer have free will to make conscious choices in this area of our life. Some triggers are really severe and truly traumatic and require professional guidance to overcome. If you have had an experience like this, you are encouraged (please!) to seek appropriate support. However, if your triggers are not like that but are more garden variety, you can definitely learn to deal with them. You no longer have to be controlled by wounds. You no longer have to impose on yourself repeated suffering based on a past event. You can be free to respond to the world, yourself, and those around you with conscious choices.

Now that we have some common language and definitions for energy, vibration, movement, the energy body, and energetic harmony, we can dig deeper into these ideas. You may have been told that you are not the center of the universe. That may be true sometimes, but right now you actually are the center of the universe, and if your center isn't healthy, chances are things around you aren't either. Until you get yourself in harmony, your efforts to affect the world around you will be inhibited. So let's get you in harmony!

CHAPTER 2

ENERGY HEALTH BASICS

Most people look for information about energy clearing when something already feels wrong and they want to make it right. This is possible, of course, although if you are in energetic crisis and unable to attend to your own energy due to lack of time or severe imbalance or depletion, it may be best to turn to a professional energy worker to deal with the immediate problem. Just as many people take a health scare like a heart attack as a wake-up call, use that experience to motivate yourself to attend to your own energetic health. By doing so, you will be better able to deal with crises when they occur. You may even discover that by consciously and skillfully cultivating the energy in your environment, most emergency situations can be avoided.

Before we get into more detailed explanations of personal energetic health, let's just wade into the waters of information slowly and get used to some of these ideas. We will build on the ideas from chapter 1. Our energy bodies are analogous to our physical bodies, so there will be plenty of comparisons between the two that should help clarify abstract ideas. We'll explore the importance of preventative care, the keys to energetic harmony, and the interconnectivity of all things.

PREVENTATIVE CARE
FOR THE ENERGY BODY

Successful energy clearing and effective energy cultivation is much easier when you are in energetic harmony. Sometimes people go to an energy worker of some sort and think that the session is all that is needed, that they are now in harmony—and they probably are, for a time. But energetic health, like physical health, requires constant attention. *Hygiene* is a weird word and seems odd when talking about metaphysical energy, but it shouldn't. In fact, it only makes sense that we would care for our energy body as we would our physical body; there are many parallels. Good energy hygiene is as important as brushing and flossing your teeth, getting enough exercise and sleep, and taking in healthy nourishment. There are some interesting parallels between physical care and energetic health. For example, brushing your teeth removes particles of material that are literally stagnating between your teeth and gums. Like energy, the particles are not evil in themselves, but lodged between teeth is an inappropriate place for them if we want our mouths to be healthy.

Hygiene is not the only aspect of regular maintenance for the energy body. Exercising and sleeping are two related but opposite states for the body. Both provide benefits beyond the physical. Sleep and exercise are essential not just for physical but also for mental and emotional health. Technically there are types of exercise that expend energy (such as aerobics) and types that replenish energy (such as chi gong). There are times when we use or project our energy and times when we contain or conserve our energy. Nourishment gives the body what it needs to replace cells and fuel the body. The type we take in will affect, in both the short and long term, the overall health of the body. This is similar to energy cultivation; we make choices about the type of energy with which we wish to nourish our energy bodies.

The more we learn about the requirements of our own energy body, the easier it is for us to understand what we need, as well as what we need to eliminate. We all get to learn about our own energy bodies because, just as with our physical bodies, we have some similar needs and some unique ones. Some people need more sleep than others. Some people don't feel in harmony with too much high-vibration energy, while others find it invigorating. Most of us have a few deeply entrenched energy habits that aren't serving us and that, in fact, may be increasing the gap between our behaviors and our values. Rather like the nearly continuous course correction of airplane pilots, continual care is an important foundation of any other energy work you wish to accomplish.

KEYS TO ENERGETIC HARMONY

Clearing, energy expenditure, and energetic nourishment are three key areas to energetic harmony. Clearing is the removal of energy that is not serving us. It could be energy that is making us feel unwell or encouraging behaviors that keep us from living our ideals. Energy expenditure concerns the energy we express, manifest, or put out in the world. Energetic nourishment, just like physical nourishment, is the energy that we take in consciously or unconsciously. One is not more important than the other; rather, they all work together to create a healthy whole that is more than the sum of its parts. When all areas are working in concert, we are more likely to respond calmly, thoughtfully, and in ways that express our values to the world around us, to our internal thoughts and feelings, and to others. Our will is under our control, and we are making choices we want rather than being manipulated by out-of-control, imbalanced energy.

When energy is not clear, it is like something is there that shouldn't be. Using the physical body again as a metaphor, let's say you have a toothache. Infection is where it shouldn't be, causing physical pain. When you are in pain, it is much harder to behave from a place of grounded centeredness. The body can heal by taking the steps to remove the infection, and it is easier to respond rather than react. Likewise, if you have an emotional block or destructive mental loop, you will be out of energetic harmony. You will learn how to identify and remove these energetic blocks so you have more freedom to live as you choose.

When you have expended an excess of physical energy and haven't slept, it is also easy to be controlled by circumstances. You may react with annoyance or even anger at things that wouldn't normally bother you when you've had enough sleep. If you expend your metaphysical energy without replenishing it, you have less control of yourself. For example, living in a situation that feels dangerous and where you always have to be on guard is draining. If you don't have practices that replenish your energy body with nourishing energy, you won't be able to behave as you wish or be at your best.

Finally, if you don't take in the right energy, you can feel sick, just like if you've skipped your fruits, veggies, protein, and fiber and binged on pizza and ice cream instead. It's like that story about the little boy who tells his grandfather that there are two wolves inside him fighting and he doesn't know which one is going to win. The grandfather tells him that the one that will win is the one that he feeds. You have different kinds of energy. Which will predominate? The answer depends on which you feed. An important part of energy work is knowing what type of energy you need and how to cultivate it.

EVERYTHING IS CONNECTED

In addition to clearing, controlling, and cultivating energy, we have to attend to these states for each aspect of the energy body: mental, emotional, and boundary. While it is necessary to examine them individually, it is also important to remember that they do not exist in isolation but rather work together, dependent on and supportive of each other. When one area is out of balance, all areas suffer.

The mental energy body takes in energy in the form of ideas and thoughts. If your mental energy body has collected some inappropriate energy, it can blind you to the truth or the reality of a situation. Have you ever felt like a thought has created a loop in your mind and you just can't stop replaying it? I know I have. It's important to deal with these thoughts quickly because they can become bigger problems. These obsessive thoughts existing in the mental body can become thoughtforms. Thoughtforms are ideas that have grown to the point where they have a life of their own.

You are not your thoughts. You have thoughts and you may take them up or discard them according to your will; you are not obliged to cultivate every thought you have. In the Christian tradition, priests ask people in confession whether they "entertained" evil thoughts. That idea of entertaining thoughts always seemed funny to me as a kid, but now I know it is an important idea to understand. If a thought comes to you, you can let it go or you can invite it in, make it comfy, and bring it milk and cookies. If you let it stay long enough, it can become attached to you.

Thoughtforms are no longer simply thoughts that can pass through your mind but entities that have come to roost in your mental body. The thoughtform controls and influences your mental energy body in ways that take away your free will and that cause you to react rather than respond. Remember when I said energy isn't good or bad, but it can be inappropriate or stagnant? We may wonder, then, is a thoughtform bad? That's a harder question because a thoughtform is more than just energy; it's more like an entity that you create, often unconsciously, in your mental energy body using energy. The energy used to create it isn't good or bad, but the way you've shaped it and the role it now plays in your life is often not healthy and does not promote energetic harmony.

To see how the energy aspects work together (or don't work together), let's look at an example. Let's say you have a thoughtform that says if you ever relax while your partner is working or doing chores, then you are a lazy, no-good slacker, and your partner is definitely judging you harshly. One evening you want to sit in a cozy armchair and read, but your partner wants to clean out a closet. Your partner doesn't ask you to help and doesn't mind at all if you prefer to read, but that thoughtform is screaming in your ear. One result is that you are too annoyed, defensive, and shamed to relax, so you decide to go and "help" your partner—but you bring that annoyed and defensive shamed energy with you, so the time spent together is likely to end in your partner wondering what your problem is, the two of you snipping at each other, or even an argument.

Your emotional body knows that your partner loves you and would never think those awful things about you, but it has been neglected, drained of energy that has been redirected to feed the ever-ravenous thoughtform. In addition, the thoughtform causes a rent, or tear, in your energy body boundary, making it harder for you to control what comes in and what goes out. You are no longer choosing of your own free will what type of energy enters your energetic body; rather, you are being force-fed the type of energy that the thoughtform needs to thrive.

Everything is connected. All this might seem like it would be so much work and incredibly time consuming. Don't worry. There is more of a time investment in the beginning. Once you've stabilized your energy body, you will be able to tell when you are out of balance in the smallest way and easily deal with such matters. After all, brushing your teeth or doing a monthly breast self-exam is neither a difficult thing nor a huge time commitment. Small daily or monthly practices are easy and effective in maintaining energetic harmony as well as physical health. They can even save your life, which is quite a payoff for such a small investment.

MICROCOSM AND MACROCOSM

We've mostly talked about energy health and harmony in terms of your personal energy. We understand the importance of preventative care, which can be developed through simple daily habits. We know that through energy clearing, expenditure control, and nourishment we can become energetically robust. We've explored how when one aspect of ourselves is out of whack, we cannot operate as a whole being. We also took a side trip to learn about thoughtforms, an unfortunate effect of poor energy hygiene.

Remember that principle of correspondence? As above, so below; as below, so above. All of these ideas apply to the energy harmony of spaces and places, too. Once you attend to yourself, you will be able to use these ideas to cultivate the energy around you and maybe even help others. Now that we have a shared understanding of vocabulary and general principles of energy work, the next section will get into the nitty gritty of stellar energy management, so get ready to shine.

PART 2

PERSONAL CARE

Before going further, make sure you have a journal or notebook handy. As you try the techniques presented in this section, keep good notes so that you can remember what works for you and what doesn't. There will be questions and exercises along the way that will help you to develop your own personal energy practice. These questions and exercises will build on each other, revealing what you need to know for creating energetic harmony in your life.

WHY IT MATTERS

There are many benefits to excellent personal care. We will focus on two. One is our own inner confidence and ability to express our soul's purpose. The other is being able to take up our responsibility for the creation of the world and the reality that we live in. In this section we will develop energy management techniques and dive deeply into personal energy clearing.

We humans have such a hard time finding our balance in terms of self-care. Sure, there are times when circumstances require us to limit our own self-care temporarily in order to attend to a crisis or important event. However, if we look at our everyday normal habits, most of us probably fluctuate between self-neglect and self-indulgence. That is, we do not maintain any consistency in terms of caring for our own physical and energetic needs. Instead, we ignore our needs of healthy diet, adequate exercise, and restful sleep, to say nothing of the less tangible needs of our energy body during times of high stress. Then, whenever the stress lifts, the crisis is averted, or the event is over, we indulge and self-soothe (some may say self-medicate) with activities that feel good (on some level) but do not actually replenish our reserves with the kind of nourishment our bodies and souls most want.

It's easy to see how we get into these cycles. Our culture definitely isn't designed to support balanced, healthful practices. It feels like I've been harsh on our culture a lot already and there are definitely some problems with it, but there are plenty of positive and wonderful things about the world we live in, too, so let's take a moment to honor some of the things we are grateful for. It doesn't do any good to throw the baby out with the bathwater. However, despite all the good things we enjoy, we can all discern aspects of our culture that make it harder to experience well-being. We are encouraged to worship at the altar of constant busyness, and the person who is the busiest gets to be the high priestess or something. There is no need to go into the problems with being too busy; we've all read the articles and have experienced it firsthand. We know that busyness means there is little time or energy for self-care. Then we are pushed in the other direction, being told that as a reward for all our hard work we deserve a treat, an indulgence, a little something to take the edge off and relax into mindless entertainment.

Our culture doesn't encourage or support physical or energetic harmony, and we are not going to change that overnight. Although we may dream of an ideal culture that makes it easier to live a healthy life, we have to take action and make decisions within reality. Complaining about how hard it is to find five minutes to clear your mind or about the idiots texting while driving is not helping (and, in fact, is actually strengthening those realities). Instead, we can make our health a priority, doing the things that keep us in harmony despite the problems arising in our daily lives. By doing so, we may just discover that, despite our culture, at least *our* lives can turn into something that can support energetic harmony.

Have you ever noticed that when you think you *should* want to do something or behave a certain way, it is so easy to find reasons why you can't? On the other hand, when you *really* want something, nothing can stand in your way, and you will find a workable solution to every potential problem. For me, the most difficult step is making up my mind that I want something enough to prioritize it. If I can do that, I can achieve almost anything, and I bet the same is true for you. Unfortunately, that mechanism—whatever it is inside us that flips the switch from thinking that we *should* want something to *actually* wanting it—is a mystery to me. Life would be so much easier if we could just flip that switch. Since we can't, does that mean we are at the mercy of these uncontrollable switches? Not at all. Although it may not be as immediate as hitting that magical sweet spot, we can take baby steps toward the switch. As that grandfather told his grandson, it's all a matter of which wolf you feed.

Why is it so important to take care of yourself on an energetic as well as a physical level? Probably there are lots of reasons, but let's talk about two very important ones. First, if you are not attending to your energetic health, then you likely don't know your own energetic center, your own truth, and your own boundaries. Without this knowledge, it will be more difficult to make decisions about what actions to take, what words to say, and what to keep out of your life.

You simply can't be your best self, live your values, or express your soul's purpose in the world with any kind of conscious control unless you can find your center and manage your energy.

Assuming that your interest in energy work is to create change in the world—to clear troublesome energy in your home, for example—you essentially want to move energy. The best way to shift external energy with any precision and effectiveness is from a strong foundation, when it is easier to sense a deep connection to the well of energy that makes up and is part of the universe, and you can see and express your morals and values. All of this— foundation, connection, and clarity—allows you to have confident expression and control of energy.

The second reason to value personal care goes beyond your immediate life and out toward our shared reality. One Hebrew creation story says that God did not finish creation. He left it purposefully unfinished and invited humankind to participate in the universe's ongoing unfolding. This idea is also part of the law of attraction, which teaches that we co-create reality with the universe. In shamanism there is a strong tradition that all beings (not just shamans) are responsible for the ongoing creation of the world. Even science has similar ideas, such as the expanding universe, relativity, and the effects of the observer on outcomes.

We are responsible for ourselves. We are also responsible for the world we live in; we helped create it through our actions in the physical world and through our energy work (whether conscious or not). Until we are in energetic harmony and have learned how to move through life continually course-correcting, our participation with the ongoing creation of reality will not be based on our free and conscious will. Because we won't be mindfully creating, we will either be supporting a reality that we think is inherently unhealthy or we will be adding to the movement toward disorder.

Taking care of yourself as a physical and spiritual being affects more than just you; it affects all that is. It is important work. You are worth it. We are all worth it.

Taking Note

Now it's time to pull out your journal to reflect on some questions and explore some ideas. These may not be the most fun musings, but they are necessary. We are beginning to open to the areas within ourselves that will benefit from energy work. That means identifying problem areas. This work is intensely personal. No one ever has to see what you write in your journal. Be honest with yourself.

1. What are your values as you understand them right now?

2. Write out your schedule for a normal day.

3. Write out your monthly budget.

4. How are the items in question 1 reflected in the lists from 2 and 3?

5. Based on 2 and 3, what might someone assume your values are?

6. What parts of our culture or society do you value? How do you support those aspects?

7. What parts of our culture or society do you wish were different? How do your actions help change them? How do your actions continue to support them?

CHAPTER 3

ENERGY-CLEARING TECHNIQUES

The physical world is a great metaphor for the metaphysical world, especially if you keep in mind the principle of correspondence: as above, so below. We can look at any number of physical entities—a garden, a closet, a whole house, a business, the body—to understand the concepts of clearing, containing, and cultivating. Because energy (both physical and metaphysical) is meant to flow, it is, unless inhibited, always moving. The physical world has structure and if we want the structures to remain healthy and intact, we have to take care of them. Without attention and care, things (matter, energy, systems) naturally move from order to disorder. Our nicely organized closet will change from order to disorder unless we put things away where they belong. A garden full of seedlings will produce better if weeds are not allowed to creep in. A business with a clear vision and a sound mission will lose its focus if other ideals or values are pursued. If not given enough sleep or food, our bodies will fall apart. Each of these processes—clearing, containing, and cultivating—play important roles in maintaining harmony. They are vital, but they are not difficult.

In the next two chapters we will look at the general principles of clearing, containing, and cultivating. While very important, they are refreshingly simple. In chapter 5 we will see how to apply these concepts to our energy body. These ideas are suggestions based on experience and study. By working with energy,

I've developed a template that can guide you, allowing you to fill in the spaces with ideas that resonate with you or spark your creativity, leading to your own ideas. Work with energy at your level of understanding.

I believe that energy is part of the Divine. It is not out to trick you or trip you up because of some ritualistic loophole. There are basic principles governing how energy flows, but once you understand those, don't be afraid to follow your intuition, your creative impulses, and your own common sense. We are all made of energy and are perfectly able to understand and work with it. In this and the next chapter you will be invited to try some of the practices as you read. This is to help you start learning what it feels like to attend to your own energy. Think of this time as a sampler. Start small. You shouldn't have a huge goal in mind or attempt to clear anything that you know is big and complicated. This will relieve pressure and allow you to focus on the practice itself and how you feel. Chapters 5, 6, and 7 will take you into deeper levels of this work. Chapter 8 will help you pull it all together in a personalized practice.

CLEARING

Have you ever tried to plant a new garden into untended ground or attempted to organize an overfull closet with all the stuff still in it? Both activities can be done—unfortunately, the job will be harder than necessary, and we won't be able to work as effectively. Clearing the new garden bed of rocks and roots, and removing clay or sandy dirt, will make it easier to place the seedlings or seeds in even rows and will make room for the addition of nutrient-rich soil. Emptying a closet helps you to see everything in it so you can more easily make decisions about what to keep, move, or discard. An empty closet allows you to see the space available so you can make the best use of it. These physical examples are good metaphors for energy clearing.

It isn't hard to apply these ideas to our energy body. Sometimes we say that we have to take a break or go for a walk to clear our heads. If you've ever felt that way, you have recognized that your mental energy body was filled with thoughts that needed to be sorted through. Walking helps ground agitated energy. Once that energy is cleared, it is easier to see what is on your mind. As you walked, you probably examined different ideas, discarding some and examining some more closely. You discerned which to keep and which to release.

Clearing your energy body is just like that. You consciously examine what is residing within you. Then you can decide what you want to keep and cultivate and what you want to release based on your free will. Most of us have a lifetime of energy built up like plaque on teeth or in arteries. Our energy bodies could look like a hoarder's house, so full that it is hard to move around and where stagnation is the order of the day. This is why clearing takes a little more effort and time when you first begin this work. There is an accumulation of energy that needs to be sorted.

Energy clearing is not something we do just once. It is an ongoing activity. Because most of us are not educated in good energy maintenance, as we walk through our days we are bombarded with other people's energy in the form of thoughts or emotions. If we could see all this churning energy that is not being managed but just flung all over the place, it would probably be like walking through a strange metaphysical stew. Your energy body is sticky and things cling to it. If you don't practice good energy hygiene, you will experience other people's random energy clinging to you without you knowing it. That energy then affects you, perhaps even changes you, in ways that you aren't conscious of and haven't chosen.

The regularity of energy clearing will vary from person to person. Extremely sensitive people or people who haven't strengthened their boundaries might need a daily practice. Others who have stronger boundaries or whose circumstances help them manage their environmental energy more (such as those who live alone or work from a home office) may only need a weekly or monthly practice of clearing. No matter what rhythm of habit you eventually settle on, you may also include unscheduled clearings as needed, such as if you've just had a particularly intense experience or have been in a situation that was energetically fraught.

There are many, many ways to clear energy. One is not objectively better than the others. The ones that are best are the ones that work for you. The most important aspects to consider when selecting a clearing method are whether it resonates with your belief system and is something that you will do regularly. A technique from a culture that is very different from yours might not be the best choice because it doesn't fit into your understanding. If it is too complicated or time consuming, or it requires you to purchase hard-to-find or expensive items, you are less likely to do it consistently.

For example, there are formulas for ritual baths that can be used for clearing. Some require the addition of oils, crystals, and salts as well as the use of candles. If you don't have relationships with the energy (some would say the spirit) of the suggested oils or crystals, have no interest in them, and don't even like baths, then that practice is certainly not the best choice for you. However, if you love baths and have a wonderful collection of oils and crystals that you've worked with, then this technique is perfect for you.

In addition, you may find that you prefer specific clearing practices depending on what you are clearing. For example, you may find that a more physical clearing activity, such as dancing or walking, works best for when your mental energy body is overloaded but realize that meditation is more helpful when your emotional body is cluttered.

Let's look in more detail at possible clearing techniques. They will be more like templates so that you can easily fill in the blanks in ways that make sense to you. Options and suggestions will be included, but remember, this is not a set system. You are not required to follow any particular instructions. In fact, if in reading these ideas you are inspired to create your own technique, so much the better. Your energy body is as personal and unique as your physical body. You get to decide what is best for it because, in the end, you and you alone are responsible for it.

CLEARING PRACTICES

Energy-clearing practices or techniques can be any activity that allows you to release unwanted energy. They create space in both the physical body and energy body. Because they create space, it is good to follow them with a cultivation practice so that you are controlling what will fill the space you just created. Some clearing techniques more rigorously focus on breaking up stagnant energy and should definitely be coupled with another action to release the energy you just loosened; these techniques will be noted and suggestions given for pairings. Likewise, some, particularly the earth-based ones, focus on gathering chaotic energy, which can then more effectively be cleared.

All of these techniques can be used or modified for clearing objects and spaces, as you will see in part 3. As with so much metaphysical work, intention is as important as the action itself.

While doing any energy work, make sure you are focused and your mind isn't wandering. You want to be in control of what you are doing. Just as important as intent is only doing what makes sense and feels right for you. Running is a great exercise, unless you have bad knees, in which case swimming might be a better alternative. Likewise, burning sage is a great way to cleanse yourself or a space, but if you have smoke allergies, consider a movement- or water-based technique. A big part of energy work is being responsible for understanding yourself, your energy body, and your needs. Experiment, pay attention to results, and develop the perfect technique(s) for you.

As you read through these, make notes in your journal (or mark up this book) about ones you'd like to try. Knowing what doesn't work is important too, so also note things that aren't likely to be a good match. Even these early thoughts and decisions will help you start creating your own practice. Unless there is a reason to not try a technique, I'd encourage you to do so. The more you try, the more you'll learn.

1: Movement

Movement is a great (and easy) way to move energy around or break up stagnant energy. Movement can be subtle or vigorous. We will talk about both. Mountain pose and yin yoga are gentler forms of movement, good for clearing out any energy that is vibrating too highly for your comfort. Dancing and walking can be either slow or vigorous and therefore are easily adapted to suit your needs. We will look at standing, walking, dancing, and yin yoga as clearing practices.

MOUNTAIN POSE: Yoga's mountain pose might seem like more of a non-movement activity. However, the act of assuming and holding the pose includes subtle but important movement. You don't simply stand; you stand with intention. Place your feet about hip-distance apart. Rock from your toes to your heels, finding the edges of the sides of your feet, and then settle your weight into the middle of your feet. If you were making a footprint, your foot would be perfectly and evenly represented. Tighten your leg muscles so that your kneecaps lift up and your thighbones push back. Lift your rib cage up off your waist, making lots of space for your lungs to expand. Lift your shoulders up toward your ears and roll them back and down. Make sure your ears, shoulders, hips, and ankles are aligned. Keep your chin level and lift the top back of your skull, creating space at the top of the spine. Take a deep breath in, letting it infuse your mental energy body. Release the breath and release the energy into the earth through the soles of your feet. Repeat as many times as needed to feel clear.

WALKING: When done with intention, the simple act of walking is also a wonderful practice. For me, walking is particularly effective when my mental energy body is clogged. That "all up in my head" feeling can happen after a long bout of writing or planning, listening to a deep lecture, studying or reading, or even after an intense conversation. Begin by standing in mountain pose for a few breaths while you focus on your intention, then walk, maintaining the good posture you established in mountain pose. With each step, feel the energy that you are focusing on break up and begin to move down to your feet. As your feet meet the ground, release the energy to the earth. Walk until you feel clear.

While walking try to maintain a strong, aligned posture. Also pay attention to what your body is doing while you are walking. Our bodies are a great source of wisdom and can tell us a lot about our energy body. Do you find your shoulders hunching forward as if your body is trying to protect the heart center? Are you bending forward from the waist, inhibiting your sacral or gut area? Bring your attention to those areas and see if there is other energy that needs work or attention.

Because walking is so good for moving intense or stagnant energy, I like to pair it with a simple cultivation technique. Repeating a mantra, either out loud or in my head, is my favorite. I choose one that invites the energy I want or a thought I want to replace the thoughts I released. For example, if my energy is out of whack because my car broke down and needs an expensive repair, I could take a clearing walk to release the anxiety and repeat to myself one of my all-time favorite sayings, which is from the fourteenth-century mystic and theologian Julian of Norwich: "All shall be well, and all shall be well, and all manner of thing shall be well."[4] Also, walking to clear anxiety due to a car expense has a poetic irony that I'm sure somehow supports energetic harmony.

---

4   Father John-Julian, *The Complete Julian of Norwich* (Brewster, MA: Paraclete Press, 2009), xi.

DANCING: Dancing is a natural energy mover. There are all kinds of dancing, as well as reasons and venues for dancing. Dancing at a party or in a club can be part of an energy practice—I know it was certainly cathartic for me when I was younger. Sometimes it is hard to work in a night of clubbing when we need it…and for some, that kind of venue wouldn't feel right. I've danced in clubs, at parties, at weddings, in ritual, in ceremony; with formal steps and with riotous abandon. I think any kind of dancing can be part of energy maintenance.

For me, the best energy dancing happens when alone. There is no concern about anything else (clothes, other people, whether my friends are having fun, etc.). Just pick a song and move. Learning to trust your body and its wisdom can take some getting used to, but it is worth it and easy once you get the hang of it. It isn't easy to explain how, and getting past the awkward stage (if you have one) is a good reason for dancing alone. You can experimentally move your body and see how different motions and rhythms feel. The more you do it, the more natural it becomes.

Unlike most of the other practices, while I set my intention before beginning, with dancing I don't really focus on anything after I start. In the walking practice I deliberately focus on my feet hitting the earth to release energy. Dancing is more primal, and I've learned to trust my body. Sometimes these less consciously controlled methods are great choices, especially when you aren't really sure what is wrong or where it is wrong. You just know something's got to move, so you trust your body to do what it needs to. Through paying attention during your dancing and reflecting on the experience, you can learn about what was going on so that in the future you will have that experience and that knowledge to apply when necessary.

YIN YOGA: Westerners often engage in activities like tai chi and yoga for the physical benefits. However, these practices are deeply rooted in energy work. In their entirety they clear, contain, and cultivate. Consequently, when practiced mindfully, they are awesome for energy health. Regarding clearing specifically, yin yoga is magnificent for this. Yin yoga focuses on holding passive poses for long periods, generally from one to five minutes for beginners. Physically, these long poses go beyond our larger, more visible anatomy and attend to the deeper anatomy. Long poses, particularly deep hip openers, also have an effect on the emotional body, allowing for the release of deeply held stagnant energy. If you've never done this before, go slowly and be prepared for an emotional as well as a physical experience. While I highly recommend yin yoga, any yoga is helpful for releasing because so many of the asanas create space in the body. Because of our principle "as above, so below," this space is also created in our energy bodies.

As we move our physical bodies, we move our energy. Stagnation is extreme, prolonged, and inappropriate stillness. Anxiety is intensely vibrating energy. Your body can help maintain the appropriate vibration for you in almost any circumstance. Keep stagnant energy and anxiety out of your life and keep your energy clear and flowing by moving your body appropriately.

2: Sound

Using sound is a simple way to move energy by raising vibration, creating space, and breaking up stagnant energy. While this technique is mostly used for physical spaces or while doing energy work for others, you can also use it on yourself. Remember, intention matters. Traditional methods of using sound to affect energy include rattles, drums, gongs, bells, singing bowls, and clapping. Technically, you could use singing or chanting, but I find those more effective for energy cultivation. While it is lovely to have a special instrument for your energy work, you don't have to buy a fancy rattle or drum. You can put some dried beans or popcorn kernels in a covered container, like a plastic storage container. You can use a book or tabletop to drum on.

When I use sound for clearing myself, I often incorporate movement and then follow the clearing with stillness and silence, breathing out the activated energy and consciously breathing in a light vibration such as peace or grace. Sounds can wake up the mind and our energy. When you feel lethargic, make a little noise to wake up your energetic body.

3: Water

Water is a wonderful and refreshing tool for clearing. We will talk about the easiest method, washing, as well as how to create and use infusions. Water can be used in creative visualization as well, when actual water isn't handy or when you need a deeper dive, so to speak.

WASHING: The simplest technique is to wash your hands or face with plain water. Sometimes that isn't enough, so a full bath or shower is better. While regular tap water works just fine, many people like to infuse their water to enhance its ability or create it for a specific purpose.

INFUSIONS: Adding essential oils is a common way to do this, but make sure you know what oil you are using and why (and make sure it is safe for contact with skin). While lavender is really popular, it is more a cultivating oil because it soothes and heals. I find the energy of rosemary is great for clearing. Please note that some people have a sensitivity to rosemary, and it should not be used by pregnant women. My personal favorite, though, is clary sage, although it is not typically prescribed for clearing and should not be used by pregnant women. If you have favorite oils and check them out first for safety, try them. Even though there are common prescriptive uses, we all develop our own relationships with the spirits of the oils.

Placing a crystal in a container of water and letting it sit for a few days can infuse the water with the qualities of the crystal and thereby support your clearing work. I use a black quartz crystal that a friend found in Russia and gave to me. Make sure you research whatever you want to use because a few crystals do leach into the water. Safety first!

Salt is a great natural cleanser, so you can simply dissolve salt into your water to boost its clearing abilities.

Solar and lunar infusions are also popular. These infusions are easy to make. Simply put water in a container and leave it in the sunlight or the moonlight for a while. I put water in a lidded jar and leave it on a windowsill. For a solar infusion, I leave it all day; for a lunar infusion, I leave it overnight. I tend to use solar infusions for clearing and lunar for containing and cultivating, but that reflects my relationship with these heavenly bodies.

Think about your own relationship to them and decide which is more appropriate for you. Depending on how interested in astrology you are, you can even refine the purpose of the water by paying attention to what sign the sun is in or what sign or phase the moon is in. Traditionally, a waning moon is used for releasing or clearing.

Whether you are just washing your hands or your whole body, another way to cleanse with water is to use soap infused with oils or herbs known for their clearing properties. I've found some lovely soaps infused with sage, sweetgrass, and cedar to be extremely effective. There are lots of oils that have cleansing properties. If you can't find soap with your favorite infusions, perhaps a local soapmaker could create a custom blend for you or you can try making it yourself. If good safety precautions are used, making soap is easy and satisfying.

VISUAL MEDITATION: Visual meditation is a useful and versatile method for clearing. There is so much room for imagination here, so let your ideas run wild. Knowledge of chakras is not necessary for energy work, of course, but even a minimal understanding of the chakras can be useful. Chakras are energy centers in the nonvisible body. The idea comes from many Eastern traditions and has been embraced by many Western energy workers. The word *chakra* comes from the Sanskrit, meaning "wheel" or "circle." While there are many chakras, most Western practitioners focus on the seven main ones: crown (violet), third eye (indigo), throat (blue), heart (green), solar plexus (yellow), sacral (orange), and root (red). If you Google "chakras," you will find many good images that show their location and the energy and issues that they represent.

One of my favorite general self-clearing meditations that involves water is to lie down, close my eyes, and visualize my energy body and my chakras. I begin at the bottom, with the red root chakra. I see it clearly in my mind and then set it spinning. I move up the chakras, moving from red to orange to yellow to green to blue to indigo to violet, keeping them all spinning at the same time. Then I imagine a swoosh of water coming through the top of my head (through my crown chakra) and moving through each chakra in turn, cleansing them as it goes. The water flows back to the earth to be redistributed as needed. I admire my shining, sparkly clean spinning chakras for a moment and then settle them back down. That's it. Easy as can be and so incredibly refreshing.

4: *Fire*

Fire can be a powerful clearing ally. You can incorporate fire in your energy-clearing work through actually burning things, through candle work, and, as with water, through visualization. Because it is so powerful it can be dangerous, so always, *always* be sensible and careful.

BURNING: The most common way I use fire is to write down the energy I want to release on a very small piece of paper. Using a set of tongs I have for this purpose and a cast-iron cauldron (any fireproof receptacle will do), I hold the paper with tongs and light it using a long-nosed lighter or a candle and let it burn in the container. If I were a really careful and diligent person, I would bury the ashes in the ground. Sometimes I do that. Sometimes they stay in my cauldron until the next cleaning... especially in the winter because the ground is too hard to dig.

CANDLE WORK: Another way to use fire that I've heard of but haven't personally tried is to burn a small candle, putting all the energy that you want released into the candle. To put the energy into the candle, hold it in your hands. Center and ground. Focus on the energy you want to release. Feel it leave your body and enter the candle. You can seal it by using a toothpick or other small, pointy object to write the name of the energy you are releasing. Watch it burn until it is gone. Depending on the candle, it could take a good while. If you don't have a small candle, I would dedicate one candle to this purpose and mark it in small increments, using one increment per cleansing session.

VISUAL MEDITATION: As with water, visual meditation with fire is another way to incorporate this powerful tool into your cleansing repertoire. I suggest visualizing a bright white glowing light instead of regular flaming fire. After getting comfortable in your meditative state, visualize a glorious white light surrounding you, engulfing you like a loving embrace, as you take a long, slow, deep inhale. Allow it to permeate your energy body and all the way to your core. Hold your inhale for a few counts and release it, along with the light that is taking with it all the energy that you have released. This practice, which takes only as long as a slow inhale and exhale, can be done at any time. For example, I don't know about you, but when stuck in traffic it is sometimes challenging to maintain a nice, calm harmonious energy. Giving in to the urge to be angry or swear or yell at people (as if they are on purpose trying to create traffic) may relieve feelings for a minute. Unfortunately, the aftereffects to yourself and others in your vicinity aren't worth it because all you've done is fed the chaotic, confused, frustrated energy already present. Instead, this quick and effective practice of breathing in and out with the light can make your and maybe others' drives a little less frenetic.

5: Air

Air is one of my favorite clearing elements, not because it is somehow the best out of them all but because it is a good match for me and how I work. If you already have an affinity for an element, that one may be your best medium for clearing. If you are unfamiliar with or have little experience working with the elements, try them all and see which feels most natural for you. Unless a practice really resonates and feels natural, you are unlikely to do it with any consistency, and consistency is important in any kind of practice. The techniques here include smudging, breath work, and organization.

SMUDGING: Incense is commonly associated with air, and the fragrant smoke from burning herbs or resins has been used for cleansing energy for centuries. In fact, most people interested in clearing energy start with sage. It is the most popularly given advice and has become part of mainstream culture. Burning sage is indeed a great way to clear energy. It is one that is part of my regular home-clearing work.

By the way, when reading about working with sage, you may see the phrase "smudging ceremony." The word "smudging" sounds like it might imply using the ashes; however, it really means to pass something through smoke or to pass the smoke over and around something. It is the smoke that purifies. Using a sage bundle or stick incense, light the end, let it burn a few moments, and blow it out. The end should be glowing red, with smoke coming out of it. Move the smoke over and around the item, space, or person to be cleansed.

You can use loose incense on a charcoal or electronic burner, too. Using herbs on these, though, creates a lot of smoke, so be prepared. I usually use sage when clearing spaces—you'll find more information on this in part 3.

BREATH WORK: For personal cleansing with air, breath work is incredible. We already mentioned breath work a little in the section on working with fire, so you know how easy it is: no tools are required, and it can be done anywhere without anyone even noticing. Well, they may notice a complete transformation in your demeanor, words, and actions after you've cleared yourself, but that just means you were successful. Again, as with many of these practices, breath work can be used for containment and cultivation, too. Here, though, we are focusing on clearing. The key here is emptying yourself and creating space. This means that while you definitely want to take long, slow, deep inhales, the focus is on your exhale, the release of energy. When using breath for clearing, follow these steps:

- Inhale for a count of three.

- Exhale for a count of five.

- Hold your breath (or, more precisely, your *lack* of breath) for three to five counts.

This final hold creates the space necessary to give stagnant energy room to break apart and to create room for other energy to help move it along. Do these long, slow, deliberate breaths a few times, using your inhale to help break up stagnant energy. After your final round, hold your lack of breath for as long as you can—no longer than five counts. You do this to enhance the creation of space, to experience the emptiness. This space is now available for you to fill, so as you take in your next breath, consciously choose what you want to bring in (this, too, is cultivation, but it is hard to have an exhale without an inhale).

You will find breath work in the section on cultivation (see pages 74–75). It is really one of the best and easiest tools we have. The exhales release energy, and we can use the inhales to nourish our energy bodies with what we need.

ORGANIZATION: The last air technique is particularly helpful for clearing the mental energy body and for people who feel overwhelmed by their work. I classify it as an air practice because I associate this element with communication, logic, and order (among other things). While it may be normal for people to be "at work" all the time, via their email and smartphones, we know it isn't healthy and does not increase productivity, even if it feels like it does. This practice may feel unrealistic and will take time and discipline to accomplish. I don't tell you that to make it seem harder but to make sure you have realistic expectations. Even though it took me a while to get here, this one practice—which, again, is part containment and cultivation as well as clearing—has visibly changed my life significantly. Here it is: at the end of my work week, before I shut down for my weekend, I clear my emails, clear my computer desktop, and clear my actual desktop. Crazy, right? Who has time for that? You're so busy! I know; me too. The benefits are amazing, though. You can leave with a clear mind. When you come back, you do not start your workweek with chaos. You have control over your workspace and the work itself.

There are lots of resources and articles about how to do this, but I'll share a few of my tips. For my emails, I do not use them as visual reminders to take care of something. Back in the day when I'd have a hundred or more emails in my inbox, it just created anxiety and a sense of "busy-busy-busy" that can be really addictive but is definitely not harmonious. I create folders for projects and put the emails there. When I'm ready to focus on that project, then I attend to the emails. If the email is not project-related but still requires a reply, I have a folder for those as well. For anything time sensitive, I make a pop-up reminder in my email program.

The same goes for my desktops. Everything gets put away so the visual chaos is gone and a sense of order prevails. Along with a daily to-do list, a good running to-do list helps make sure nothing falls through the cracks. As above, so below. Approach this project with calm energy, and that energy will flow through it. Keeping things clear and neat will flow back to you, maintaining a nice, complementary practice that benefits your work and your energy body.

Related to clearing the work area, something that I struggle with is keeping my phone clear. I'm not very good yet at deleting apps I no longer use, texts that are weeks old, emails that are no longer necessary, and voice mails that I was saving "just in case" but never listened to again. Oh, and let's not forget photos. Have you ever wanted to show someone a photo on your phone, only to have them sit there growing more impatient while you scroll through three hundred images? Sometimes I take a dozen pictures of a thing, person, or event, hoping that one is just right, intending to go back and weed out the ones that aren't just right. The thing is, I hardly ever do. Then, when I go to my photos to actually refer to one, anxious energy rises up and is not pleasant to experience; it also makes it difficult to find what I'm looking for. The good news is that I'm slowly getting better at this.

You see, maintaining a healthy energetic life is always a work in progress. The nice thing is that once you establish a system and practice it consistently, it eventually becomes second nature, so you can move on to the next area without feeling overwhelmed. Organization and clearing work wonders in both the physical and energetic worlds.

6: Earth

When you are feeling scattered or flighty or are in a very reactive state, earth-based practices are just the thing. For stagnant energy, though, I suggest using the other practices. Earth is good for settling chaotic energy and gathering it together so it is easier to release. Here we will discuss the benefits of working with crystals and trees, the importance of pets, and the magic of naps.

CRYSTALS: The simplest and most common practice is to carry a stone or crystal in your pocket so you can touch it whenever you need grounding. The type of stone can determine a more specific flavor of grounding. I have a few personal favorites, namely tiger's-eye or any one of a small collection I've gathered over the years while on hikes. A good crystal book or well-staffed metaphysical store or rock shop can help you and is a particularly good choice if you don't know much about crystals because you can actually hold them and see how they feel to you. Salt is such a good energetic cleanser, but, except for using it in a bath, I usually use it for clearing spaces rather than personal energy.

Like breath work, crystals are also used for cultivation. They carry specific energy within them, and luckily we are able to access it when needed.

TREES: Even though it has become a joke in some circles, hugging or leaning against (as well as sitting or standing beneath) a tree is such a powerful way to release energy. A tree feels so powerful and wise; I always feel complete trust when I ask a tree to be an ally. No matter how chaotic or reactive my energy, I know a tree can handle it. Likewise, even just going outside and touching the ground works if you don't have access to a tree.

PETS: Holding, stroking, or playing with a pet is very calming. There are plenty of articles about how these activities calm the physical body; as we know, the physical and energy bodies are connected. However, use care with this practice. Interact with the pet to settle the energy, but do not release it into the animal. Instead, after you feel settled, follow this activity with something like mountain pose or breath work to release the energy.

NAPPING: The next practice might not seem like energy work, but it is among the most effective techniques I know: take a nap. Of course this isn't always possible, but if it is, then just try it. I've long said that the most powerful magic practices I know are to tidy up (which moves stagnant energy) or to take a nap (which settles chaotic energy). When the energy of the mental or emotional bodies are worked up, sometimes being conscious is counterproductive. As long as your mind can keep spinning stories, it is easy to feed obsessive thinking or stoke already heightened emotions. Sleeping is an effective way to give the mind and emotions space to calm down.

7: Spirit

Spirit-based practices are perfect for contemplative types or those who like a more devotional experience with their energy work. Some of my favorite spirit-driven techniques include prayer and good works.

PRAYER: Prayer—or communion with a deity or however you envision the Divine—can be a simple and direct method of managing energy. In the same way I ask a tree to take unwanted energy from me and give it back to the earth to be redistributed where it is most appropriate, I can also pray to my concept of the Divine, asking it to do the same. For those who already have a prayer practice, this is a natural and easy method. For those who do not pray, it can become a simple, quiet, and beautiful experience if it suits your belief system. If, however, the act of prayer is tied to unpleasant memories, substitute meditation for prayer. They are not the same thing but are very close. In prayer we commune with the Divine, while meditation is a way to connect with our highest inner wisdom.

GOOD WORKS: While it may seem strange to couple a spirit-based approach with mundane physical-world actions, this is a powerful technique. If you know the nature of the energy you want to clear, determine an act that counters it. For example, if you want to clear selfish or clingy energy, do an altruistic or charitable act. If you need to release angry energy, forgive someone.

While most of the practices explained above are great for in-the-moment energy experiences, this one is particularly good for chipping away at long-standing, deep-seated energy within yourself. Sometimes energy takes up residence in us and shapes our behavior in ways that are not consistent with our values. While we would like a single ritual or healing session to take it away once and for all, that generally doesn't work because those behaviors have become habits. Even if the energy has been released from the energy body, the physical body (including the mind) has to catch up. It takes time for the physical body to release old habits. Consciously training yourself to behave in a way that is in line with your ideals through consistent action will create lasting change. If the behavior of the physical body isn't changed, the energy will probably return since the environment is so inviting.

Now that you've learned some clearing techniques, you'll probably want to learn ways to keep everything nice and clean. Containing your own energy is important so that you do not get depleted. Further, once you've gotten rid of what doesn't serve your true purpose, you don't want it coming back and taking up residence. Let's look at some methods that can help us contain all this good energy we've worked hard to clear.

Taking Notes

Before moving on, make some notes about your reactions to some of these techniques. Try at least one from each section. Note the energy you felt before the technique and how the energy changed afterwards. It is important to keep good notes because although we always think we will remember everything, unfortunately we just don't. Your journal will become an important tool as you learn about energy work and develop your own personal practice.

1. Which seem like ones you'd never use? Why?

2. Which are you looking forward to trying? Why?

3. Of the ones you've tried, which surprised you the most? Why?

CHAPTER 4

TECHNIQUES FOR CONTAINING AND CULTIVATING ENERGY

After clearing some of the stagnant or inappropriate energy you've been carrying around, you will want to contain and protect your energy body. Containing is simple and easy. Once you have enjoyed the spaciousness of your cleared energy body, you can practice cultivation. Bringing in specific energy is one of the great benefits of energy work.

CONTAINING

Containing practices focus on the boundary of your energy body, which is like the skin of the physical body. These techniques are used both to contain energy you want and to keep out energy you don't want. The boundary of the energy body is permeable and sticky. We are, after all, one with all that is, so it can feel like everything wants to stick to you even if you don't want it to. These things—energy in the form of ideas or emotions—aren't *all* inappropriate, but because this is your energy body and because you have free will, what you keep is your choice. As a human being and fellow co-creator of the universe, it is your right and your obligation to discern and decide what stays and what is released.

For many people, especially those who identify as sensitive or empathic, containing can seem challenging. If you are one of those whose energy body seems particularly magnetic and sticky, you may often feel overwhelmed by emotions and energy that are not your own. Consequently, developing at least one containing method will help you feel freer and more purely yourself.

The same can be true for those who may not be extremely sensitive but instead have lots of contact with many people, whether in person or in other ways, particularly in any online venues such as social media, in any comments sections, or forums. Very few of us have a clear concept of energetic hygiene. Because of that, our energy is all up in each other's energy and nobody is clear on whose is whose. No wonder life sometimes feels like a big confusing mess. Containment helps you know what is yours to deal with and what is not yours to mess around with.

1: Bubble of Light

This is a common practice because it is both simple and effective. You can do this technique seated, standing, or lying down. Close your eyes and focus on your inner core. Imagine a flame igniting and burning white, bright, and strong. Charge this flame with the task of protecting your energy body. Determine that nothing will permeate or attach itself to you unless you permit it. Encourage its light to expand until it fills your body. Once your body is filled with this light, push it through your skin in all directions, infusing your energy body. You can start each day with this practice or simply employ it whenever necessary. It is especially effective in situations where there is a lot of energy flying around—for example, heated meetings, fraught social or family gatherings, or unpleasant social media interactions are excellent times to cloak yourself in light. You'll feel more like your true self and be able to share your light and help others.

2: Cording

Perhaps a better name for this is *de*cording, because that is what this shamanic-inspired technique feels like. It is technically both a cleansing act (as it removes something unwanted) as well as a method of containment. We've mentioned how sticky our energy bodies are, but that is not the only way that energy finds its way in. A cord is an energetic connection between two people, a person and a place, a person and a thing, a person and a group, or a person and an idea. The cord is not only a connection but a conduit that allows energy to pass back and forth between the two ends of the cord. The energetic give and take is not always equal. Someone can attach a cord to you that siphons your energy or infuses energy to your energy body.

There are a few ways that we develop cords. First, when we have a relationship with someone, something, some place, a habit, an emotional wound, or an idea, we develop a cord with it. A second way that cords develop is when someone attaches one to you, even if you aren't in a relationship. As an author and teacher, this happens to me frequently. The people sending the cords aren't necessarily doing it with malicious intent. Admiration, gratitude, and respect can form cords as well as jealousy, annoyance, and disgust. Whether well-intended or not, we operate best when we are conscious and in charge of our own energy, so even these kindly meant attentions can have unwanted effects. A third way cords are formed between you and something else is when you are reaching out energetically and attaching to someone or something else, usually unintentionally, although sometimes we do it on purpose. A version of this is when a relationship ends and one person isn't willing to let go. They keep trying to re-establish a cord with their ex.

Removing cords has been such a useful practice in my life, and I hope it helps you, too. It is not hard to do. In the beginning, you may find it helpful to do this once or twice a week, but after you've established a good foundation of energetic harmony, once a month will probably work well. It is impossible to be completely decorded every minute of every day—or if it is possible, I've not discovered how yet. This technique is best done while standing. You are going to remove the cords and let them dissipate, with the energy within them being absorbed back into the earth to be redistributed as needed. I usually feel and hear a soft sucking noise, as if a suction cup is being removed. You will do three rounds. The first round of cords includes the ones that represent mutual relationship. The second round focuses on ones others have sent to you. The final round is for ones that you've sent out. Here are the basic steps, which you will repeat three times:

1. Stand in mountain pose and close your eyes.
2. Imagine your energy body, in your mind's eye seeing it and all the cords that are attached to it.
3. Starting from the top of your head and moving toward your feet, mentally pluck the cords and drop them.
4. After your third round, finish either by imagining the points of connection healing over or with the bubble of light practice from page 64.

As you decord, you will notice that some are slender and wispy while others can be quite large and gnarled, especially when you first begin the practice. That's because those cords have been fed and cultivated for a long time. I've found that most cords can be removed easily. For the most part, I don't try to identify every cord that I remove. With cords that are larger, it may take more work to completely eliminate them. You may have to gather and direct more conscious and focused intention and energy toward them.

When I first learned this technique, I didn't think that completely decording was wise. After all, I wanted to maintain my connection to my wife, my family, and my friends, didn't I? Upon reflection, I realized that while I do want to maintain connections with loved ones, energetic cords were not the way to do it. In order to be in healthy relationships, you need to be a whole person. You need to manage and own your energy, and the other people have to do the same with their energy. Sharing each other's energy is a form of co-dependence. It is easier to keep relationships clean when we aren't mixing up our emotions and stories with someone else's.

Remember that cords are like hollow tubes creating a channel between you and another person. Energy flows back and forth through the tube. This flow can be unconscious or conscious. That is, someone can actually drain your energy or send inappropriate energy your way. Like the energy we are talking about (and, as a matter of fact, like chakras), cords are not physically visible.

Decording will not devastate your relationships, unless, of course, they were unhealthy to begin with. Strong, loving relationships will only benefit from one or ideally both people being independent beings who have control over their own wills and energy. Release the ties that bind, free yourself and others, and you may just find that you are closer to your loved ones than ever.

3: Namaste Hands

While this name may seem silly, it is the most descriptive. Whether you've practiced yoga or not, you've probably seen at the end how the practitioners put their hands in a prayer position and say *namaste*. Why do they do that? As a casual yoga practitioner, I admit there are probably some deeper, more meaningful reasons that I don't know about. What I do know is this: in yoga there is an emphasis on both clearing and cultivating the space and energy within the body. After putting in the effort to release what isn't needed and inviting in what is desired, placing the hands in prayer position—hands flat and palms together in front of the heart—completes a symbolic circle. The active and receptive hands form a closed circuit so that whatever was released stays on the outside and whatever was cultivated is kept inside.

This is a quick and easy technique to use after any clearing or cultivating practice, but it can be done at any time. If putting your hands in prayer position would be awkward—for example, in a meeting—you can simply clasp your hands together under the table. The most important element is that the palms are touching. This metaphorically expresses the idea of nothing coming in and nothing going out because the expressive and receptive centers in the palms of your hands create a single continuous barrier. Traditionally, the left hand is known as the receptive hand and the right as the expressive hand. However, you may prefer to reverse that if your left hand is dominant.

Simply by closing your hands, you close the circuit, keeping your energy just as you want it.

4: The Metaphor of Skin

The skin is a metaphor for the energy body's boundary because they both inhabit the same space and perform similar functions. This is similar to how the heart chakra, while invisible and non-physical, inhabits the same area and has attributes similar to the physical heart. Your energetic skin is permeable, just like your physical skin. Unlike your physical skin, your energetic skin is also sticky. It contains, protects, and gives form to your energy.

You can intentionally treat your skin as the physical symbol of your energy boundary and use specific oils or herbs to protect it. Salt is cleansing and it is also grounding, which is a form of protection. A salt-based scrub used with intention in the shower or bath can help protect your energy boundary. Add a boost or more specific intentionality by adding oils or herbs that support your desires. As always, do check for health and safety issues before using any oil or herb on your skin. Reference books can help if you don't have specific preferences. I encourage you to keep it simple. There is no reason to go buy lots of expensive or exotic oils and herbs. Cedarwood and lavender are among my favorites for protection. Rose oil is commonly used; however, I do not care for that scent, so I cannot speak to it personally.

Salt scrubs are not the only way to apply scents to the skin. Lotions made with essential oils are useful, too. In my hometown there is a shop that sells soaps, lotions, candles, and oils. They have unscented versions of everything they sell and will customize whatever you want with the oils of your choosing. Select oils that you associate with protection or grounding, trying different blends to see how they smell and how they feel energetically. You could take this idea even further and drop a small crystal in the bottle to infuse the lotion with those qualities in the same way as a water infusion. As an added benefit, beyond energy containment and having soft skin, catching a whiff of the scent throughout the day will help remind your conscious mind to pay attention to the energy around and within you.

Your skin is your largest organ. It is both strong and delicate. Take care of it so that it can take care of you.

5: The Power of Yes and No

The proper use of the words *yes* and *no* are imperative to good energy containment. Energy containment focuses on the energy body's boundary, and these little words are important tools for determining and maintaining your energy boundaries. When you say yes to something, you are agreeing to expend your energy on whatever was asked of you. We all say yes too often, usually out of fear of upsetting someone else or a sense of obligation or guilt. None of these are reasons that support our values, unless your life values are to make sure no one is ever upset but you or that you always do what others expect. Before saying yes to something, make sure it is in alignment with your beliefs and values. If it is not, then use a strong and confident no to honor your energy and your soul's purpose.

Saying no may be one of the hardest things you learn to do. I know it was (and continues to be) difficult for me. In the fall of 2016 I was working on two very large projects, with another following right on their heels. These projects require a great deal of creative energy, focus, and time. My tarot reading practice also requires a big investment of energy, attention, and, of course, time. During this time I chose to honor the spirit of these large projects by devoting all my resources toward them. This meant shutting down my reading practice, at least temporarily. It was a hard decision but the right one. Harder still, I had to personally say no to former clients who wrote to me, even though my website clearly says I'm on hiatus and there are no buttons for booking readings. However, being able to devote myself to important projects has been a benefit to both the work and my own energetic harmony.

This does not mean we can say no to whatever we don't feel like doing. Energy work and cultivating your spirit requires responsible discernment, not childish indulgence. You and you alone are responsible for your energy. Make sure your yeses and nos consistently close the space between you and the values you want to live by. As in all things, there are pros and cons to being a mature, healthy person. Use your words in ways that express your authentic soul's purpose.

After clearing out energy that doesn't serve your life's purpose and developing ways to keep it safe, you'll probably feel really good. Many people have a sense of lightness, focus, reduced anxiety, even deep peace. It is really amazing to realize how crushing it was to carry around all that unneeded energy. Relish those sensations and know that you deserve—indeed, were designed—to feel that way.

While this is very wonderful, it gets even better. Now that you've made some room in your energy body and learned how to manage your boundary, you can cultivate more of what you want. That's when things get really exciting. Energy cultivation has been, at least for me, like a snowball. I start off with this little kernel of desire, feeding it as well as I can, keeping it safe. It grows exponentially and fills me with this glorious potential that I never knew could be mine. The really cool thing is that it is not difficult and the results are fast, so it is easy to stay encouraged and continue your practices.

Taking Note

1. Which containing techniques are you looking forward to trying? Why?

2. Is there one you'd never attempt? Why not?

3. What do you think of saying no to something that doesn't serve your values?

4. Consider vowing to respect your soul's purpose this week by saying no to something that isn't in line with your values but that you would ordinarily may have accepted due to guilt, fear, or obligation.

CULTIVATION

Clearing and containing are important and necessary. Cultivation would be pretty useless without a clear base and safe space to keep the new energy. But I have to admit that cultivation is my favorite part of energy work. Perhaps it is because I am a maker at heart...and really, all humans are makers. We are born manifestation machines, and even as children we experience the pride and excitement about whatever it is we've made. With cultivation practices, we select the energy we want to manifest in our lives and in the world. Then we nurture it, which includes eliminating anything that diminishes that energy and encouraging anything that strengthens it.

When cultivating in a clear, contained energy body, we have the opportunity to create ourselves. Cultivation is a creative act. I purposefully use the word *cultivate* rather than *maintenance* because maintenance implies maintaining a status quo. As human spirits having a physical experience, we are meant to always be in movement, always changing, always reaching toward our ideals.

Energy work in general is incredibly active because we are constantly freeing and re-creating ourselves. The space between your old self and your new self—which is to say, this very moment and every moment—is the space where you get to create your future self and also influence the future of the world.

They say that the past affects the future, and it does. But the past is just as malleable as the future. We get to choose the story we tell about our past, and examining those stories is a part of good energy work. We get to plant the seeds for our future. Also, because my ideas are based so heavily on the principle of "As above, so below," these techniques often benefit both our mundane/physical lives as well as our energy bodies.

Some of the points discussed below differ from the sections on clearing and containing. The previous sections describe actual practices that can be applied in many different circumstances. Energy cultivation requires an even more individualized approach. The categories presented here describe powerful ideas for cultivating energy. They provide you with topics to explore that you can use as you develop your personal cultivation practices. Specifically, we'll discuss how what you consume, both physically and mentally, is connected to energetic harmony. The things we own play a role in energy work. We will see how chaos and gratitude can be useful tools. Finally, we will reveal the importance of consistent practice and the power of your mind. But first, we'll look at two basic practices, breath work and crystals, that we first talked about in the clearing section. They are simple and effective and a great way to start cultivating the energy you want right away.

1: Breath Work

We've already discussed breath work, so we don't have to go into too much detail. As you know, the exhale is used for clearing energy. When we cleared, we held the exhale. Now we are cultivating, which is drawing in energy, so we will focus on the inhale. It is wonderful to combine both clearing and cultivating with breath work because they really do go hand in hand. You can clear energetic space and then immediately fill it with what you need. For example, you can exhale anxiety and inhale peace.

Before you begin, identify the energy you want to cultivate, or invite into your energy body. This is where focusing on specific energy rather than simply "good" or "bad" energy comes in handy. You are training yourself to cultivate exactly what you want.

When using breath for cultivation, follow these steps:

1. Exhale for a count of three.
2. Inhale for a count of five.
3. Hold your breath for three to five counts.

This final hold brings in the energy you asked for. Do these long, slow, deliberate breaths a few times, using your inhale to help break up stagnant energy. After your final round, hold your breath for as long as you can, but no longer than five counts.

2: Crystals

As with breath work, we've already talked about the benefits of crystals. Just as some are really great at clearing or grounding, others have wonderful energy that you may want to bring into your life. A commonly used crystal is rose quartz, said by many to radiate loving energy. I've used citrine to cultivate joy and abundance. Moonstone has been great for intuitive development. Again, a good crystal book or just spending time with a few crystals will help you identify which ones will bring the energy you seek.

Using a crystal for cultivation is easy. Simply carry it in your purse, bag, or pocket. You can sometimes find jewelry made with various stones, which is decorative as well as practical.

3: Intentional Consumerism

This is a broad topic, so we'll be spending a lot of time here. We live in a world that has taught us that our most important function is to consume. It's almost impossible to break away from that identity, but we can start by paying more attention to what we bring into our lives physically, mentally, and energetically. Think about everything you consume, and ask yourself if it is benefitting the energy that you want to thrive or if it is actually creating or feeding a different type of energy. In other words, does the consumption of the item bring you closer to living your values or does it create distance between your actions and your beliefs? As you consider the energetic nutritional value of something you are thinking of consuming, don't forget that where and how it was created is as much a part of that item's energy as the thing itself. That is, the methods of production and their consequences are in that item's energy makeup.

Let's just start right away with the thing that is on everyone's mind—the elephant in the room: media, both social and corporate. We are all familiar with social media, whether you've participated in it or not. By corporate media, I mean any kind of news, marketing, or entertainment, whether visual, audio, printed, or online.

Imagine everything that you consume—and if you just glance at a hateful meme on Instagram, you have consumed it—as particles of energy that attempt to permeate your energy body. The sheer amount of stimuli we subject ourselves to every day makes it difficult if not impossible to maintain our boundaries and keep our energy bodies clear. Imagine the quality of the energy that any particular stimulus is providing you. As you scroll through headlines and images, it may seem like each individual one is so small that it couldn't possibly have that much of an effect on you.

The impact is cumulative. You can use this to your advantage by curating your media consumption thoughtfully, with an eye toward feeding the energy that you want to cultivate. If the stimuli that you are subjecting yourself to is mainly inflammatory, black-and-white, willfully ignorant, and shallow, is that really nourishing the energy that best expresses your soul's purpose and values?

I've had some interesting discussions with people about the role of news in our lives. When I say that I stay away from most news sources, many of my friends and family protest, saying that to be a good citizen, one must stay informed of everything that is going on in the world. I agree, but I define "good citizen" as one that is actively involved in the shared life of our society.

Most of the people in my life who say they obsessively take in the news are only passive consumers, not active participants. They watch or read and then get very, very upset about whatever it was someone did to someone else. They've taken in a headline and story that were purposefully devised to create as strong an emotional reaction as possible, so they've taken in the poison and have reacted to it. It has become part of their energy body unless they clear it. Most of us don't clear it…or we say that when we vent or rant about it, we are clearing. That is not clearing. That is spreading that energy further through the world. To me, that is not being a good citizen. If you aren't sure whether you are a good citizen or a passive consumer, try this experiment.

The next headline or story that gets you really worked up or causes you to express a mean or judgmental comment, make a note of it, either on paper or electronically. Put the note in your calendar to be opened three months from now. I do this often with Outlook, my email program. It allows me to create tasks that pop up on my desktop on a certain day. When you open the note that pops up in three months, add to that note all the ways in which you actively did something to help the situation or ways in which that knowledge influenced your behavior. Most of us will find that after ingesting the poison and perhaps spreading it around, we've done absolutely nothing. In that case, staying informed has done nothing positive for us or for the world. Be careful and be thoughtful—and, above all, be honest—about what media you are consuming and why.

As you avoid things that would be poison to you, make sure to carefully curate the things that you take in, selecting those that nourish you. Your selection process should take into account not just the content or subject matter but also the method of conveying the message. One of the pitfalls of our current environment is skimming rather than diving deeply. Instead of reading a book about something, we graze on headlines and tweets. FOMO, or "fear of missing out," drives us to consume at wild levels for fear of being the last to know something. The sad thing is that these headlines and tweets and such are designed to trigger reactions rather than invite thoughtful responses. They exist to keep you in a constant state of anxiety and upset without providing enough facts or critical analysis. It is like our mental body is forced to exist on junk food—just like a physical body on such a diet, the mental energy body becomes flabby and the muscles of our discernment fall into disuse. Find a well that will nourish you, and drink deeply from it.

Another danger of taking in so much uncontrolled media is something we discussed earlier: thoughtforms. If you take in enough of any specific energy, it can take up residence and exert its will, limiting your free will. Or worse, rather than becoming a thoughtform—which is, luckily, a separate entity—the energy can permeate your energy body and change you in ways that you haven't consciously chosen and that are more than likely not a true reflection of your values or a fulfillment of your soul's purpose.

Media is not the only kind of consumption that affects the energy body. The physical products we purchase or acquire have energetic ramifications internally and externally. Externally, when we support corporations or companies with practices that do not match our core values, then we are moving away from our values toward theirs. The action of you buying items from companies creates a cord between you and that company. Further, you've used your energy to support and nurture that company's goals and actions.

When I think about all the stuff I buy each year, I'm overwhelmed. It is such an important responsibility and so complicated. It is almost easier to think "Oh, I can never figure out what is what and what companies share my ethics, so I won't even bother." That is the approach I took for years. Luckily, I've discovered another way to look at things that is less overwhelming, more realistic, and, most importantly, moves in the right direction, even if it is just a baby step. Once per quarter I pick something, just one thing, that I intend to change about my purchasing habits. Only doing one change every three months gives me time to figure out the practicalities of the change and time for the change to become a habit before I move on to the next change. It also gives me time to figure out all the implications of the change.

For example, a recent shift for me involved the food I eat, in particular meat and eggs. I don't eat much meat, so it didn't seem overwhelming and the transition went very smoothly; it isn't hard to find ethically bred and sourced meat. However, about six weeks in, I realized that I was buying the same deli meat as before because for some reason, deli meat didn't seem like meat or something. Once I was aware, I made that change in my buying habits. Giving myself enough time to integrate a change helps things feel less stressful, allows me to be more thorough and make changes to the plan as necessary, and, finally, shifts the change into a true practice.

Not wanting to support corporate farms that commit atrocities on animals was the external reason for changing that particular practice. In this case there was also an internal reason. My wife was on a road trip through Kansas and learned about the feedlots. I never knew what they were, even though I'd heard the word before. They are places were animals are fed and kept the last few months of their lives before they are killed. It sounds as if those last months are simply horrific. I can only imagine that the meat coming from animals who experienced such a life and death would be filled with the misery of their existence. This may be all crazy talk, but it feels real to me. I didn't want to eat misery. So in addition to supporting companies that share my values, I am, at least in my mind, bringing in energy (both physical and metaphysical) that nourishes my physical body and my energy body in what seems like a more appropriate way for me.

Food consumption is an easy thing to change, especially if you only take on one specific type of food or one food group. It has the benefit of supporting both internal and external energetic goals. But food is not the only consumer choices we make. Anything that you purchase or any service you hire can be examined and possibly changed to be more in line with your goals. Besides media and food, clothing is the other area I've made such changes. If clothes are made in ways that exploit people or deplete the earth with no regard to replenishing it, those items carry that energy. You wrap your energy body in the energy of these clothes. As much as possible, make sure that energy brings the quality of nourishment that you want to consume.

A few areas that I'm nervous about addressing are hair care products and art supplies. I share this to let you know that this is not an all-or-nothing practice. Any steps, no matter how small, are beneficial and will have larger ramifications in the long run. It's not always easy and we are never perfect, but we can always move toward becoming the people we want to be. You don't even have to be perfect to write a book on the subject. We all are in this together, finding our ways and helping each other as best we can.

Very often, perfectionism is an insidious concept, causing us to feel defeated or to simply give up. As a devoted chaser of perfection for most of my life, I know what a burden it is. More importantly, it rarely supported me in achieving my personal best in a graceful way. That fun fact about airplanes really struck a cord. Remember, when an airplane is in flight, it is off-course 90 percent of the time; the other 10 percent of the time is spent in course correction. This means that the amount of time spent precisely on course is zero, yet the planes almost always arrive where they were headed. We can take a lesson from this story. Our ideals and values are the destination we want to reach. The journey there will not be smooth and perfect. Instead, we train ourselves to use a light and loving hand when we course-correct our thoughts and actions as we move through life.

4: All Your Things

We do love our things. Sometimes we love them for their beauty, usefulness, or sentimental value. Sometimes we love them because we've been taught to love them. We are told to work hard in school so we can get good jobs so we can buy all the things that make life worth living or prove how successful we are. We'll consider what our things say about us, how we care for them, and why we acquired them in the first place.

Let's face it: our relationship with our things is complicated. We've had many decades of being taught that more is better and the newest anything is superior to the older version, unless it is a rare antique and costs quite a lot. In fact, these days most consumer items are designed to be replaced; this helps keep the wheels of capitalistic consumerism spinning. As it seems to be

reaching a fever pitch, an interesting trend is gaining popular-
ity and traction: minimalism. So the pendulum swings from one
extreme to the other as some minimalists compete for who owns
the fewest items.

With ownership of things, as with most situations in life, a
healthy balance serves us best. The number of things you own is
completely up to you; there is no ideal set number that promotes
the best energetic health. Instead, it is up to individuals to think
about the energy of the items they acquire and determine not only
if that specific energy is nurturing them in a way that moves them
closer to their ideals but also how those items interact together.

Looking at the big picture of your current possessions, what
story might someone tell about you? Someone with lots of clothes
and personal-care items but very little in the way of books, music,
culture, and hobbies could be focusing all their energy into external projections and neglecting to nourish their inner life. Someone who lives surrounded by piles of books and papers but with
bare cupboards might be putting all their energy into their mental energy body and neglecting the physical world, which is as
important as the energetic; indeed, everything is connected and
has value. So it is not only individual items that affect our energy;
the sum total of our stuff creates the energetic environment.

Starting with the big picture, try to see what story your stuff is
reflecting back to you about yourself, your beliefs, and your ideals.
If any one area stands out as a problem—as being not in line with
your values—then that is a great place to start. Ask yourself why
you've devoted so much money and space to these things that
don't reflect the person you want to be. Determine what you can
let go of or what sort of energetic clearing you can do so that you
are able to let go of it. You may find that you release an entire collection of things or a significant number of things in that group-

ing. After the initial area, move through your home, car, and work space looking for groups of things that don't fit who you want to be, and use them as an opportunity to learn about yourself, your wounds, and your assumptions. If you are doing this work as you read along, be careful not to get too extreme and purge right away. At this point you are simply bringing your awareness to the issue. As we move through the book and learn more about specific areas of cultivation, we'll develop specific techniques to carefully curate our environment.

A healthy environment will vary from person to person. But remember that energy is meant to flow, so any place that is too full can encourage stagnation. The amount of movement can vary by individual and by where we are at in our lives. I had a friend who rented out a tiny apartment in the lower level of his house. It is partially below ground and rather womblike. It felt more like a safe place, without a lot of energy flowing in and out but not stagnant either, just very slow and gentle. For the several years he'd been renting, he noticed that the renters were always women who had just left a long-term and difficult if not abusive relationship. They stayed long enough to heal and then moved on. For them, that space was perfectly appropriate in that moment.

On the other end of the spectrum, if someone wants to invite change and move their life in a different direction, releasing items that are attached to the old life and creating plenty of space for new energy to come in would be more appropriate. With energy work, there are not very many actual rules that can apply to everyone in all circumstances. It is best to develop your own skills in understanding and managing energy so that you can make the right decisions for where you are and where you want to go.

The things that you surround yourself with matter in and of themselves. How you treat, care for, use, and think about your things matters, too. Each item has its own energy. You have your own energy. Just by being near each other, you affect each other. How you interact—the relationship you have—is itself a type of energy cultivation. Do you treat your things with care and respect or toss them about, letting them become dirty or broken? What does that say about how you value the energy that the item is bringing into your life? Why would you have items that you don't value enough to care for? In the realm of energy work, it is not just what you have but how you have it that creates your ultimate energetic environment.

There are plenty of reasons why people don't think much about how they take care of their belongings or even mistreat them. One obvious reason is that things are designed to not last very long either materially or in terms of what is fashionable or, as they say, "on trend." We can easily address this issue by asking ourselves if disposable items bring us closer to living our values or push us further away.

Another reason could be that we experience deep disappointment in the item because it was sold to us as something that would change our lives and it didn't. Marketing relies very heavily on this notion that a physical item can change your life completely. Of course there are items that can change your life— central heating, for example, or eyeglasses. But these wonderful items don't change the whole of your life. They do not guarantee complete happiness. Things, no matter how wonderful and actually life-changing, will not make your overall life happier. In our search for happiness, we want to believe that the right jeans, boots, perfume, car, coffee maker, etc., will fix what is wrong. That puts unrealistic expectations on the item, which is the fault of the marketing team, not the thing itself. If you are putting unfair expectations on the things in your life, try instead to identify the true source of need in order to find what can actually fulfill it.

5: Consciously Applied Chaos

Most energy work is geared toward creating a peaceful, calm, stable environment both internally and externally. We know from personal experience and from the study of neuroscience that this middle vibrational ground is usually the optimal place to operate from. We are better able to take in facts, see the bigger picture, and respond rather than react to situations. We also know that there are times when we need to withdraw to be alone and quiet with our own thoughts, feelings, and energy. Even when living in a carefully cultivated, stable state, occasional bursts of chaos encourage creativity, increase problem-solving abilities, and show you things from a different point of view. You don't have to be suffering from stagnation to employ carefully crafted bursts of chaos. In fact, adding the unexpected to your life from time to time can actually be part of keeping your calm energy from turning stagnant. By consciously deciding to do something a little differently, you are inviting in Trickster energy.

Trickster is an archetypal character found in myths and stories from all times and all places, and Trickster represents, among other things, the element of chance, luck, surprise, and chaos. When we consciously invite in this energy, we are less likely to be blind-sided by it. If we get too staid, sometimes the universe sends in a little kick to help shake us up. We may not always prefer the universe's choice of how or where in our lives to apply that energy.

Instead, think about bringing it in yourself, in specific ways and areas. Artists do this all the time by trying different sorts of challenges, like using only a set number of colors, using random drawing prompts, or trying new techniques or mediums.

You can do this in simple ways. For example, if you always take a walk around your neighborhood in a certain direction, reverse or alter the direction. This may sound silly, but, at least for me, it actually works. I walk my dog around a lake near our house. We always go counter-clockwise. There is no reason. We just started that way and never changed, until one day I thought it would be interesting to see what it felt like. It was a little uncomfortable at first, but then it was invigorating. All day I was inspired to look at things from a different point of view.

Try it yourself. Take a different route to work. Write a paper letter instead of an instant message or text. Try a completely different exercise or yoga routine. Read a book in a genre you don't usually read. Part your hair on the other side. Wear two different socks or two different earrings. Sit in a different chair or spot on the couch. Whatever you decide to try, do it consciously; pay attention to your energy and see how it shifts. Through experimentation, you'll find ways that you can use now and then when you need to shake something up in a precise manner.

6: Gratitude

Most of us have heard about the dramatic power of gratitude, and many of us have seen its effects either in our own lives or the lives of others. I have a friend who practiced writing out at least three things she was grateful for every Friday for two years. She kept herself accountable by emailing her list to me each week. As the months went on, there were usually an average of ten items. She began the practice at a time in her life when things were falling apart, and she just needed a life preserver to hang on to until things calmed down. But even after she found herself on surer footing, she kept at it because the benefits were palpable.

I've mentioned the Hermetic principle of correspondence more than once. The law of attraction is also a useful principle, when understood and not used to justify consumerism or escapism. It explains why a gratitude practice is so powerful. It is not so much the actual items that you focus on and feel grateful for; it is the act of expressing gratitude. When your energy vibrates at a level of gratitude, you invite more opportunities to express that gratitude. By cultivating gratitude, you learn to see the world through different eyes. You learn to find the blessings in everything.

7: The Power of Small, Consistent Actions

This idea has already been mentioned, but it is so important that we should spend a little time with it. Just like we don't brush our teeth, eat, exercise, or sleep only once in our lives and call it good, we don't clear, contain, or cultivate our energy body with one single action. Energy—in general, and our energy body in particular—is a living entity, and, as such, it needs consistent attention in order to thrive. Even though this point is under the heading of "cultivation," it really includes clearing and containing. When everything is connected, it isn't always easy to compartmentalize certain aspects. Compartmentalizing is really helpful in breaking down complex ideas and explaining how to do things, but it is easy to overplay that hand even when it isn't the best way to serve the ideas. In its broadest sense, cultivation includes clearing and containment.

Our lives are so very busy that the idea of adding one more routine to our schedules or writing down another task on our already overflowing to-do lists seems impossible. This is one aspect of modern life that makes energy work so challenging; it is also one reason it is so vital. The lucky thing is that energy awareness can be worked into our days very naturally, layering it onto things that we are already doing every day.

As you move forward with developing your personal energy practice, keep in mind that small, consistent actions will create larger and deeper changes more effectively in the long run than a single grand gesture. It might make more sense for you to think of your energy work as a natural, seamless part of your daily life rather than a complex daily ritual involving several techniques that takes more than fifteen minutes and must be done in a certain space at a certain time.

In fact, if you like, *don't* start with requiring yourself to do something daily. Instead, think of a repeating pattern that happens regularly but maybe not necessarily daily that you'd like to change. For example, if you suffer, as I do, from severe impatience while waiting in line or being stuck in traffic, just promise yourself that in those moments you will practice some simple breath work. Anytime you are walking, even through the corridors of your office or the aisles of the grocery store, you can release energy. Visualization can be done while brushing your teeth, washing the dishes, or folding laundry. Start with just one thing and let it slowly become part of your life. Avoid adding the stress or pressure of huge changes or actions that feel alien and unnatural. Your energy is natural. You are natural. Let your relationship with it develop naturally and peacefully. Get to know it slowly, as you would someone who will become a very dear friend. I promise you that adding just one energy technique to your life will take you in the right direction.

8: Prayer, Contemplation, Meditation

Many of the cultivation techniques presented here are externally focused because I believe that our environment is a reflection of our internal life and that it also influences our inner experience. This symbiotic relationship goes both ways. Thoughts that pass through your mind can be released to go their merry way or you can invite them in, give them your attention, nurture them...in short, you can feed them so that they grow in power and ability to affect your energy. This can work to our detriment or to our advantage. I don't know about you, but I'm super skilled at this. A random awful thought can pass through my mind, and I can grab it and force-feed it with an obsession like you've never seen before. In no time, a thousand worst-case scenarios are fully developed and rippling their anxious, fearful energy through me until it feels like that's all I'm made of. If you've ever done that, take heart because it means you have great skill and ability. With a little conscious control and discipline, you can refocus your talent toward cultivating energy that draws you closer to your ideals.

There are differences between prayer, contemplation, and meditation, but they are all practices that focus mental attention on something specific: the object of our prayers, contemplation, or meditation. I've heard yoga and meditation teachers advise that if your mind is trying to drag your attention, realize that the thoughts are just suggestions. Just because your mind offers a suggestion doesn't mean you have to take it. Instead, you can bring your attention to your breath. Whether you are practicing yoga or simply going through your day, you can decide what thoughts to give energy to and which ones to ignore. As a cultivation practice, prayer, contemplation, meditation, or even journaling give you the opportunity to consciously and carefully select an idea or type of energy and feed it.

Like so many aspects of energy work, engaging in prayer, contemplation, or meditation works both ways. As you focus on your chosen value or idea, let's say forgiveness, you nurture the energy of forgiveness in your energy body. At the same time, as you pray or think about forgiveness, you learn more about it—its complexities, its various ways of manifesting, its ramifications and possibilities. It grows stronger within you, and your understanding of it becomes more robust. Applying your vast mental energy and skills to your values is actually a very easy and effective way to cultivate the kind of energy you want in your life. We all know how to think. Not only how to think, but if you related to that idea of obsessing about a worst-case scenario list, you know how to think really well. Like the kids in the Harry Potter series who have magical powers but don't know it or don't know how to direct and control it, all you need is a little guidance, a little discipline, and a lot of practice. You can give all of that to yourself. Using your values as a guide, making a commitment to taking control of your energy, and developing a practice that fits neatly into your life, you can masterfully cultivate the energy that will serve your soul's purpose most.

Taking Note

Which of these areas for cultivation spoke to you and why?

1. Was there one that you were eager to explore?

2. Did any cause you to clench, close down, or feel afraid? I find reactions like that to be great opportunities for reflection.

Try adding just one simple cultivating act to your life. Perhaps it could be something as simple as breathing in peace while in a maddening meeting, carrying a crystal to promote loving-kindness in your actions, making a commitment to cultivating peace and ease while driving, or thinking about something you are grateful for while brushing your teeth.

Now that you have some ideas about what to do in order to clear, contain, and cultivate your energy body, in the next chapters we will talk about how to know when and why to use a specific practice. As you have seen, the practices are not difficult; knowing when and why to use them can be more challenging. You will be asked to examine yourself with honesty and compassion and might find yourself facing some fears, wounds, or triggers that have held you in bondage for years. But you are brave. You are worth it. You can do this. You were born to be free.

CHAPTER 5

PREPARING TO CLEAR

We are such complex creatures; there is so much we don't know about ourselves and how we work. This is especially true with energy work or anything metaphysical, although honestly even in Western science it is hard to get a handle on things because we don't always know what we don't know. Through study, practice, experimentation, and personal experience, we do our best to figure out what works for us. In the case of the energy body, there are so many different models and philosophies. In my experiences, there is not a concrete separation between our physical body, our mind, our emotions, our spirit, and our energy body. Everything is connected.

People have different theories about whether thoughts create emotions or how emotions affect thoughts. As with most things, the truth is probably in the middle. Emotions and thoughts can shape each other. Similarly, an emotional experience can usher in a spiritual revelation that changes our thoughts and consequently our actions. The state of the physical body, at least for me, definitely can affect my emotions or thoughts. Being able to clearly separate things out sometimes makes them easier to understand, but we should be careful not to sacrifice truth for ease of explanation. Imposing arbitrary structure on something as organic as the holistic experience of being alive can, if not used with care, do more harm than good.

chapter 5

THE IMPORTANCE OF ROOTS

While you can do any of the techniques described in the previous chapters based on your own self-reflection and intuition, you can be more precise in your work if you understand more fully what is going on within yourself at a deeper level. Going deep has the added benefit of increasing your probability of getting at the root of the energy that needs clearing. If you don't address the core issue, then you will repeat the cycle and only clear each occurrence on a surface level. The ultimate goal is to clear all your major energy issues arising from experiences in your past so that you are as free as possible from being controlled by that past.

This work takes time and dedication, but the end result means that you are equipped to deal with daily energy issues as they arise. You are encouraged to face your large issues, but I recommend that you start with smaller ones, for several reasons. Smaller problems are less overwhelming, and dealing with them provides good training for future work. As you experience successes and the benefits of small steps, you will create momentum and confidence before continuing on to more challenging concerns. For example, exploring your impatience in traffic will probably be easier than tackling an issue about your relationship with your parents.

Sometimes metaphors are helpful illustrations of abstract ideas. Imagine a very dirty house, one that is not only filled with clutter but also with years of dirt built up in nooks and crannies and coating surfaces. You can move some things around, put others away, and maybe run a dust cloth over some areas. It'll look better, but until you get all the clutter out and scrub the dirt away, it's never going to be really clean. The clutter attracts more clutter, making things you need hard to find. Life is heavy and overwhelming in such a place. Living in a situation like that is like doing surface-level energy work, such as occasionally using sage to clear yourself or your home; it will help, but it will not go deep and not last as long. However, if you sort out all the stuff and deeply clean the dwelling, then life flows more smoothly and the space is easier to keep clean.

In this chapter we'll review the benefits and goals of personal energy work. We will discuss the nature of our shadows and how they contain clues to problem areas. This will help us in the next two chapters as we learn to identify and clear our energy blocks and unhealthy cycles.

THE BENEFITS OF ENERGY WORK

The real treasure of energy work is not necessarily in making your life easier, although you will find that it does, but rather in allowing you to become the person you were born to be. Good energy work allows you to live freely and express your values. This work is transformative, using your past experiences and the wounds they caused as lessons to enrich your present self. Energy clearing brings clarity to your values, which can get buried under years of familial and societal conditioning. It saves you from following false passions by helping reveal your true passions. It helps you to both know yourself and be your true self.

Whether you think you know it or not, you do know (or at least part of you knows) who you are meant to be. The description of your ideal self is found in your deepest held values and most beloved ideals. No one can tell you what those are. As you energetically strip away all that separates you from your values, you may notice them evolving and becoming more refined. This is a common result of energy clearing. As we know, life is a journey that takes us toward our goals. The destination is not the accomplishment of those goals but rather the continued relationship between your current self and your future self. The self-reflective activity of energy work allows you to ingest your former wounds, biases, and triggers and transform them, creating the fertile soil from which your future self will grow.

Another benefit of personal energy work, in addition to living with freedom and identifying our values, is being able to trust our desires. So often we are advised to "follow our passions." Passion and desire are great ways to steer our lives. We can run into problems when we are not in energetic harmony because our passions become contaminated and therefore are not trustworthy.

In Ignatian spiritual practice (a spiritual practice centered on everyday life that was created by Ignatius of Loyola, the founder of the Jesuits), the concept is called *agarra contra,* or disordered attachment. Ignatius's advice is relevant for modern people trying to achieve energetic freedom. He taught that in order to make good decisions, ones that allow you to follow God's will (a Catholic phrase that is similar to what we mean by our "soul's purpose"), you have to identify between ordered and disordered attachments. Ordered attachments bring you closer to God, while disordered attachments pull you further away. Similarly, our energetically harmonious passions and desires can lead us closer to freedom and living our values, while contaminated ones create a larger gap. So if you've ever felt let down by the beguiling advice "follow your passion," you can reclaim it as you clear your own energy and trust your desires again.

We live in a society that lacks true initiation rites to help us transition from childhood to adulthood. Consequently, many of the traumatic experiences from our childhood follow us into adulthood. These old experiences create wounds and triggers that cause us to react rather than respond to present circumstances. Without processing and transforming these experiences through energy clearing, we are trapped in contaminated cycles of behavior that do not express our values and ideals. We are bound to the past and cannot experience true freedom.

Even when we know what traumatic events caused our issues, we often use that knowledge as an excuse for our behavior. That knowledge is not an excuse, though. It is only an explanation. As adults, it is our responsibility to understand our issues and transform them. Admittedly, this is not always easy. Wounds hurt. Past traumas were frightening experiences. Plus, it can be really hard to stay solidly in the present moment as adults in a safe place and observe our past. It takes great strength to hold back ingrained reactions and remain neutral. But we yearn to be whole and healthy, to transform our wounds and live fully and free. Transformation can come in many forms, such as energy work. Psychology, therapy, and spiritual direction are also effective methods, and people often employ several routes simultaneously. Energy work as described in this book draws on psychology, therapy, and a wide variety of spiritual ideas to create a well-rounded, effective approach to energy management.

THE SHADOW

So much of the inappropriate energy we generate and express comes from our shadows. In this section we will establish a basic understanding of the shadow that goes beyond the common use of the word. We will begin to explore how clearing it releases stagnant energy and reveals parts of yourself that have been hidden away. We will start to understand that the treasure hidden in our shadows may not be what we thought and how vital it is that we reclaim it.

In psychology we often hear or use the term "shadow" or "shadow self" to describe parts of ourselves that we have denigrated and separated from our identity for various reasons.

Unfortunately, the connotation is that *shadow* means "dark." This leads us to believe that the shadow self is the dark self and contains only characteristics that we might deem negative, such as anger or fear. A more nuanced understanding is that the shadow also contains qualities normally considered positive. So we employ the phrase "the bright shadow" to distinguish these so-called negative and positive qualities. However, deciding that we want to needlessly label and separate these qualities complicates matters and perpetuates the idea that some parts of us are good and some bad, which isn't necessarily accurate. The truth of the matter is that anything kept in shadow is going to stagnate.

Going further, the characteristics we usually identify as shadow are the results of separation and not the actual part of the self that needs integration. This is a very important distinction. We may recognize that we have trouble expressing anger, for example, and conclude that our anger is in shadow. The truth is, it may or it may not. More than likely, it is the story connected to the anger rather than the anger itself that hides the real treasure, the lost part of yourself. Whether we call it shadow work or soul retrieval or energy clearing, we are reclaiming parts of ourselves that we need to become our true selves. The recognition of the difference between the story attached to a feeling or thought and the feeling or thought itself will be important in the next two chapters.

Instead of "shadow self," I prefer the term "shadow closet," which I learned from shamanic teacher Christina Pratt. Your shadow closet is where you put all the parts of yourself that have suffered trauma. By trauma, I mean any sort of experience from small hurts to serious experiences. If you are dealing with really major trauma, you should work with a trained professional to transform those experiences. For most of us, though, we'll be dealing with more common, everyday traumas that we can handle on our own. Use your own good judgment regarding what you can manage and what you cannot.

Another problem with allowing things to remain hidden away in your shadow closet is that you were born with all the parts of yourself that you need to live your soul's purpose—that is to say, to live a life that reflects your values. One of the reasons we struggle so much with living up to our own ideals is that we are missing important parts of ourselves. Anything that is missing essential pieces, whether a thing or a person, is not going to work the way it was intended. Therefore, an important—and, I would argue, necessary—part of energy work is cleaning out your shadow closet. That is where you will find the roots of most of the reactions you have that separate you from being the person you want to be. In fact, if you truly feel that you don't know your soul's purpose (that is, you cannot identify your own deepest values), it could be that the part of you that does know has been separated by trauma and hidden in your shadow closet.

SHADOW CLOSET CLUTTER
CONTAINS CLUES

Before we dive into the intensely personal work of identifying things we need to release, let's enjoy a little pep talk inspired by Elizabeth Gilbert. In her podcast *Magic Lessons* she is talking about creativity, but we can apply the same wisdom to living our values, creative and otherwise.[5] In her podcast Gilbert helps people to discover, access, express, or develop their creativity. When people have excuses about how it is impossible to make space in their lives to honor and express their creativity, Gilbert suggests that we must fall in love with our creativity. I say we must fall in love

5   Elizabeth Gilbert, "Sexy, Dirty, Nasty, Wicked," July 25, 2016, in *Magic Lessons*, podcast, https://www.elizabethgilbert.com/magic-lessons/.

with our ideals. She invites us to remember a time when we were madly and passionately in love with someone. How often did we rearrange our lives and schedules, no matter how inconvenient, for even just five stolen minutes with our beloved? Nothing mattered more then, and nothing should matter more to us now as we seek to manifest our deepest values in our lives and in the world.

If you've been struggling to free your energy and gifts, you know that the only inconvenient thing is to *not* live your ideals. There are larger stakes here, too. It's not just about you personally. You were born with unique gifts; more than ever, the world needs those gifts you carry—that medicine only you can give. We do this work for ourselves. We also do it in service to the world. Sometimes, though, we don't feel that passionate love for the values we claim to hold. Additionally, sometimes we don't even know for sure what ideals we really hold. As you begin to clear out your shadow closet, you will remove the layers, the stories, and the lies that separate you from that clear understanding and deep love.

Your values, ideals, emotions, and thoughts are energy. Even though it is invisible, we can see its effects. We begin the search for treasures that are trapped in our shadow closet by looking for the results of that stagnating energy in our lives. These are clues. Stagnating energy creates loops of energy that manifest as repeating behaviors. Once we identify cyclical behaviors, feelings, or thoughts, we can use them as guides to find the energy that needs clearing or releasing. Our worst, most shameful, painful behaviors become our treasure maps to what is essential to living as we are meant to live: as free beings expressing our gifts in the world.

Focusing on emotional and mental behaviors may seem more psychological than energetic, but in my experience it is all connected. For those of us who are not gifted psychics, I've not learned any other reliable method for clearing personal energy. While a psychic or energy worker can help identify root problems, only you can do the actual clearing work.

Being able to define the items in your shadow closet for yourself allows you to take the initiative and repeat the work as necessary until all your vital gifts have been freed. Being skilled at clearing, containing, and cultivating your own energy makes it easier to continually take care of yourself, becoming energetically strong and robust. You will expand your comfort zone so that you are able to behave in ways that you really want to, no matter the circumstances. In addition, you will be able to notice imbalances or emerging issues more quickly, so that you can clear them before they become full-blown wounds, prejudices, or triggers. We'll start with exploring emotional clues and then move on to mental clues.

CHAPTER 6

IDENTIFYING EMOTIONAL BLOCKS

Searching for emotional clues is serious work. It takes a great deal of courage to face our darkest parts. In addition to courage, we should come to this work prepared to treat ourselves with love. Love is honest, patient, and kind: qualities that are essential for this journey. This chapter will lead you through some key ideas. One of the most important is the difference between emotional reactions and emotional responses. We will talk about the three emotional states: acceptance, denial, and indulgence. Using these clues to find treasures in our shadows, we will identify the attached stories and free the treasure. This chapter will also contain some exercises to help walk you through the process.

BEGIN WITH LOVE

To be energetically mature adults, we must be willing to be honest with ourselves. This means observing and analyzing our behavior, especially what we might think of as "bad" behavior. We need to be honest, but we don't need to be brutal or cruel. Spending time in constructively critical self-reflection can lead some of us into the trap of self-flagellation. This is something that has no place in our energetic health and is, in fact, one of the mental clues we'll explore later. For now, just remember to do this work with a loving and compassionate touch. Treat yourself the way you would a dearly loved friend. While discernment is vital, judgment is dangerous. Judgment creates criticism and separation, while discernment fosters understanding and clarity. Judgment reflects the insecurities of the judge; discernment reaches out with a desire to bring things into harmony.

If you are anything like me, you do not always emotionally respond to situations in ways that reflect your beliefs. Instead, wounds, prejudices, and triggers cause kneejerk reactions, which, at least in my case, either create an escalating situation or cause me to feel ashamed and sorry later. When I say "wounds and triggers" I am not referring to major traumatic experiences that cause, for example, actual post-traumatic stress disorder. I am talking about the excuses we make for ourselves regarding everyday-level poor behavior. Wounds and triggers are explanations for such behavior, not excuses for it. As adults, once we've identified something as a wound, trigger, or prejudice, it is our responsibility to heal and transform it. Otherwise we are simply wounded children walking around in adult bodies, sometimes armed with words and behaviors that can cause deep damage. When we move through life wounded, we are controlled by the past. Every time we engage in behavior rooted in wounds, we are revisiting the initiating trauma on ourselves.

To be loving individuals, we have to love ourselves. Loving people will not purposefully force others to constantly relive horrible experiences and let that control their lives. Clearing these kinds of emotional traumas is an act of self-love. It allows us to live more freely and with more confidence because we know that we can handle ourselves in a wide variety of circumstances and still retain our center.

REACTION VERSUS RESPONSE

One easy way to tell if you are having an emotional reaction that has an attached story is when your reaction to something is out of proportion to reality. Whether you withdraw, explode, or weep, whenever your behavior does not make sense with the actual situation or is out of line with your values, take note of it. Practice noticing these moments. Being able to see these snapshots is good training in living a self-reflective life. It is also the first step in clearing your closet. In the beginning, don't worry about trying to transform yourself right away. Let's face it: trying to sort things out while you are in the midst of an emotional meltdown probably isn't going to work, at least in the beginning.

The goal is to eventually turn your reactions into responses before acting on them. For now, just start noticing your behavior. Once you get used to that, you can work on being able to actually step back in the moment and make a conscious choice about how to respond, rather than simply reacting.

EMOTIONAL STATES

In order to identify emotional clues that can lead us to the gifts trapped in our shadow closets, we need to understand different emotional states. The three that help me understand and analyze my issues most are (1) acceptance, (2) denial, and (3) indulgence. Acceptance is the ideal state, while denial and indulgence are the keys to identifying areas that need work. Denied and indulged emotions do not exist in isolation. Instead, they are attached to stories that we tell ourselves. The emotional reaction is like a signpost. The story attached is the string that we can follow to the root cause. The root hides the treasure or gift and can require careful assessment to untangle.

Taking Note

Start tracking your emotional reactions that are out of proportion to the situation. You might ask your loved ones to gently help you with this, as we are not always aware of how strong our reactions can be.

1: Emotional Acceptance

Before we work with denial and indulgence, let's talk about acceptance. Emotional acceptance is not a flag for a problem. It is the state that we hope to achieve with our feelings by doing energetic clearing. Acceptance neither denies nor indulges emotional experiences. Instead, it is the act of allowing yourself to feel the emotion, identify it, and observe it—and, ultimately, allow it to guide you. Until we can feel, identify, and observe the emotion, it can't guide us; it can only bind us. There are two big differences between acceptance and indulgence or denial. With true acceptance there are no stories attached to the emotion and hence no judgment. Also, it is only in the state of acceptance that we actually feel the emotion.

After I started doing this work on myself, I was shocked to realize how infrequently I lived in emotional acceptance. Now that I am cultivating an energy body conducive to emotional acceptance, it is amazing how much lighter and freer I feel, even though I'm technically actually feeling more emotions. It is so sad how we live with pain for so long that we forget what it feels like to not have it. To get to this spot, though, requires a little more work and a little more pain. But the great news is that after you take care of shadow closet stuff, you won't have to keep reliving that pain over and over again. You can enjoy your emotions—all of them— as natural experiences. You won't have to feel the energy of stories and judgments that you then use to condemn yourself and that keep you in bondage.

Taking Notes

Start tracking when you are in emotional acceptance. This is important because knowing what emotional acceptance feels like helps you to identify when you are in denial or indulgence.

Recognizing emotional acceptance may be challenging at first, probably because we are less familiar with it or don't pay much attention to it. Learning to recognize it is essential, especially as we move on to denial and indulgence. Here are some tips that may help. You may be in emotional acceptance if:

1. You are fully present in the moment, without thinking about the past or the future.

2. You are naming the emotion but not judging it as either "good" or "bad."

3. You are not trying to blame or credit someone or something for causing the emotion.

4. You approach the emotion with curiosity or even wonder.

5. You don't attach a story to the emotion. Attaching a story could look something like this: you presented an idea at a meeting and it didn't meet with the enthusiasm you expected. You feel rejected by the team. You then assume that either all the others are against you in some grand way or that you are worthless. A story is like drawing a broader conclusion from a momentary emotion—a conclusion that doesn't necessarily logically or realistically follow.

2: Emotional Denial

As you develop skill in observing yourself, start identifying if you are in denial or indulging. Most of us are familiar with denying our emotions. We've been told all our lives that repressing our feelings is unhealthy, and we easily recognize the truth in this. Repressed emotions are ones that are ignored and hidden away where they can stagnate, causing even further problems than the one that instigated the repression in the first place. While there are cases where we honestly don't know that we are denying an emotion, usually we know that we are. We may not know which emotion we are denying, just that it is uncomfortable and we'd prefer to not even name it, let alone actually feel it.

We are not the only ones to notice that we are repressing something. Repressed emotions have a very noticeable energy. Perhaps someone who clearly senses that something is off asks us, "So, what's wrong? It seems like something is wrong." When we snap back, "Nothing. I'm fine," chances are there *is* something amiss and you're not fine. Other times, we may express some other emotion that we aren't actually experiencing, and those who know us can always tell. They may feel betrayed, knowing that you are lying to them by pretending to have an emotion that you actually don't.

The trouble is that we are often lying to ourselves as well. We are in denial because something about that emotion with its attendant story causes pain, shame, or fear on top of the already problematic feeling that we are repressing. The possibility of experiencing those feelings causes such anxiety that we completely shut it down, usually without knowing what the actual emotion is, although sometimes we do.

Taking Note

Begin tracking when you recognize being in emotional denial. You don't have to understand why you are or what is going on right now. If you can at least stop yourself and recognize that you are denying your emotion, that is a huge step in the right direction. Identify emotional denial by paying attention to when you claim everything is fine when it isn't or that you aren't upset when you are.

Another signpost for emotional denial is subtler and harder to pin down. As you pay more attention to your feelings, you will also be able to identify emotional denial when you lie about your feelings, substituting some other emotion for the one you actually experienced. For some reason, the emotion substituted is more acceptable to your mind. For example, I used to cry when I was mad because being sad was more acceptable than being angry.

3: Emotional Indulgence

In our culture, emotional indulgence is usually confused with acceptance, which is a neutral, observing state. Indulgence is at the other extreme end of the spectrum from denial. Because we are not familiar with this idea, we will spend more time exploring it than we did with acceptance and denial.

When we are in a state of emotional indulgence, we may be expressing a lot of emotional energy but we aren't really feeling the emotion. Instead, we are reacting to the self-judgment we visit on ourselves or the projection we place on others. These reactions are based on stories connected with the emotion. Emotional indulgence loves to find excuses or blame others for our out-of-proportion reactions. That makes it easier to ignore the work of feeling the emotion because we are distracting ourselves by acting out and pointing fingers.

Most emotional indulgence can be identified by cyclical behavior patterns. Words or phrases like "trigger," "pet peeve," "I can't stand it when someone _____," "I'm so empathic; I feel everything," "that pushes my buttons," or "she just rubs me the wrong way" are good clues that we are using emotional indulgence as a way to bypass our actual emotions. If you find yourself reacting the same way to circumstances that share similarities without regard for the differences, you are probably indulging in an emotional story bred from something in your shadow closet.

Here's an example. People with healthy energy bodies and mature egos can usually laugh at themselves. If people cannot accept good-natured teasing or see their own silliness, they often respond with disproportionate anger, claiming that they are being cruelly mocked and demeaned. Their friends feel confused because, after all, it is the same sort of affectionate joking that they all share in. The angry people, though, have a story attached to being teased that happened in their past. Instead of clearing that energy from the experience of being teased, they relive that horrible series of emotions caused by assuming their loved ones are being malicious and hateful to them. These people can never enjoy the sweet and intimate experience of being so close and comfortable with someone that they can share teasing moments.

Another way to identify emotional indulgence can be when we claim that other people are making us feel something and that we are so sensitive that everything is hurtful. You might have read or heard that we are not supposed to say "You made me feel hurt by what you said," but rather "I was hurt by what you said." But really, it doesn't matter which way you say it; the focus is still on the cause of the emotion instead of the emotion itself. The person who said the words is responsible for them, but if they really didn't mean anything hurtful, they are in a difficult situation. Feeling confused, they may say "I'm sorry you feel that way." I've seen people, myself included, in the midst of emotional indulgence get really upset at that response. The other possible response, "I'm sorry," is not the right choice, either, because they didn't do anything wrong and so the apology is, on some level, insincere. More importantly, that apology gives you an "out" from having to identify what is really going on with your emotions.

You are responsible for how you react—or, better, respond—to whatever was said. This does not absolve people from saying mean and hateful things. We are not talking about purposeful maliciousness. We are talking about situations where we take things the wrong way and run with them. No matter what is going on, you get to decide: are you going to be controlled by a past trauma and react immaturely or are you free to consciously assess the situation and respond in a way that is in line with your values and beliefs? I'm not saying that other people's words or actions never cause us to feel hurt, sometimes by intent, sometimes through carelessness. But many of us, for some reason, go straight to assigning blame for the cause of the feeling rather than experiencing the emotion followed by reflection.

For example, your spouse—who loves you best out of everyone in the world (if this isn't true, then you have a very different problem)—passes you as you lounge on the sofa reading a book and says, "Oh, weren't you going to the grocery store?" Such a benign, information-seeking question can make some people feel defensive and hurt, and behave accordingly, much to the confusion of the spouse. You shout and pout and stamp around, slam your book down, grab your keys, the angry energy pulsating off you in waves, leaving your spouse bewildered and a little scared of you. I feel safe in assuming this is not in line with your values and doesn't match how you would ideally choose to treat someone you love. How can such an innocent question cause you pain and cause you to so drastically leave your values in the dust, especially since, based on the wording of the question, you must have mentioned something earlier about doing the shopping?

Instead of pausing and asking yourself that very question, you jump straight to feeling hurt and assuming your spouse is judging you. Reflection before reacting may encourage you to ask yourself why you assume your spouse, who loves you and wouldn't judge in such a passive-aggressive way, is acting out of character.

Realizing that this is absurd and that you have assigned a wrong motive to their words, you dig deeper and recognize a pattern of behavior: getting your back up whenever anyone questions you about doing something you consider a chore. Further meditation brings up a memory of being punished and criticized by your mom for not cleaning your room by a certain time. That's the root cause, and now whenever you are in a similar situation, you jump to feeling hurt and behaving defensively because you assume that you are being harshly judged for no reason.

Following the clues back to the source isn't really hard, and most of the time when we see the root, we feel like it is so obvious. Yet, because that pattern built up via repetition for years, maybe decades, we couldn't see what was really going on. We were controlled and didn't even know it. But once you know that the story exists in your shadow closet, you can remove it and free yourself.

Here is the interesting part, and where we often get shadow work wrong. The treasure—the part of you that needs to be reclaimed—is not about doing chores when you are supposed to or about lying around whenever you want. We need to go deeper. What was it that kept you from cleaning your room that first time? Were you reading? Daydreaming? Doodling? That is the hidden treasure, the part of you that needs rescuing, buried under the trauma, the story, and the now well-established pattern of behavior.

Taking Notes

1. Make a list of things that you consider your pet peeves or buttons that get pushed. Start paying attention to when they come up in your life, and track them in your journal.

2. Notice an out-of-proportion or incongruous emotional reaction on your part.

   ❧ Question yourself about the rationality of the emotion you are feeling.

   ❧ Do your reasons (the story you are telling yourself) match reality?

   ❧ Look through your journal and see if you have other similar occurrences and can identify a pattern.

   ❧ Be as clear as you can about naming it. For example: "Whenever someone mentions my nose, I behave ridiculously."

3. Meditate or reflect on your life, trying to find the first instance of this particular situation. Ask who or what you ask for guidance—your soul, your spirit, your higher self, a deity, the Divine, the universe—that that first instance be revealed to you.

4. Look below the surface and see if you can make out the treasure hidden there.

ATTACHED STORIES

We keep mentioning attached stories because they are so import-ant. In the discussions of the various emotional states, I've tried to include some examples. Here, though, we'll take the time to explore one in more detail.

In my experience, we fail to be in emotional acceptance because we focus on the story that we attach to a feeling rather than on the emotion itself. For example, when someone critiques my work, I behave very defensively, denigrating the criticism and often the one offering the critique. Being mean to those trying to help me is *not* one of my values, yet based on my actions, you'd think that was an important value. The emotion is that fun duet of anger arising from shame because I did not do a perfect job.

The story I've attached is that if I cannot do the work perfectly, then I have no worth as a person. Now when I feel that shame, I pause and really feel it. I acknowledge it and name it. I stay there. I do not jump to the conclusion that I am worthless. How did I come to associate imperfect or perfect work with self-worth? In hindsight, it wasn't hard to discover. Being told that "it is a good thing you have brains because you don't have beauty" in an era where being pretty was the most important (and pretty much the only) thing a little girl could do played a role. Another piece of the puzzle was being punished when I achieved anything less than an A in a class. My siblings were not held to this standard. The reason I was given was, "You have great potential, and with that comes great responsibility." My only saving grace, apparently, was that I had a mind, and if it wasn't perfect, then I had nothing spe-cial to offer. At least that was the story I told myself.

Does the treasure attached to this story have anything to do with work or perfection? Not exactly. The treasure has to do with doing things to please myself. It was when I was simply doing things for the joy of it—playing dress up, trying new things with art or writing, being with friends—that I fell short of the perfection expectation, when I wasn't pretty enough or pleasing the teacher and getting an A. The real treasure isn't being able to be content with imperfect work. The real treasure is doing things that bring me joy or express a creative drive with no attachment to the outcome. The real treasure is realizing not everything is attached to personal responsibility, pleasing others, or achievements.

Old habits die hard, and sometimes there are residual reactions to being criticized. Progress is being made every day, and I am less likely to bite off the head of anyone who offers suggestions for improvement. This is a nice side effect rather than the treasure.

Emotional clues become easier and easier to identify the more you do it. While this work can feel really clunky and strange at first, it becomes smoother in time. Even more importantly, because you will start feeling and behaving so much better, you will be encouraged to keep at it. Emotions are challenging, for sure, but only because we don't have enough experience with them and because we've been so wounded. You already know enough now to make some huge changes in your emotional energy body. Now we will turn our attention to mental clues. Thoughts are just as challenging as emotions, and we can all use a little more practice in understanding the role of mental activity in our lives.

CHAPTER 7

IDENTIFYING MENTAL MISDIRECTION

Mental misdirection differs from emotional traps in some important ways, which we will discuss below. We will spend some time talking about the difference between discernment and judgment because this is key to understanding mental misdirection. One thing the mental body shares with the emotional body is that there are three states that I find helpful. Curiosity, justification, and reproach are the states we will explore in this chapter.

We use emotional clues to follow the breadcrumbs to treasures hidden in our shadow closet. In my experience, our mental energy body wounds don't hide treasures in the same way as our emotional energy body does. Instead of hiding what we need, it misdirects our energy away from expressing our true selves. It traps our attention that could best be applied elsewhere. It channels our resources away from what our souls desire. It doesn't hide a treasure but it keeps us from being able to experience or express it to its fullest potential.

As for why we have this tendency, we can only surmise. Based on my experience, it is due to our cultural and ancestral history and to the sad truth that sometimes things that feel so good to our wounded child are not good for us. Rather than having a root cause, mental misdirection is usually a habit developed to support behaviors that divide us from our true ideals. The good news is that just as we can free ourselves from emotional wounds and triggers, we can free our ourselves from mental traps and misguided channels. By clearing these tendencies, we can redirect our energy to nurture and cultivate what we actually want rather than being controlled by past training.

MENTAL STATES AND DISCERNMENT

Just as there are three main emotional states that I've found useful in personal energy work, there are three main mental states: curiosity, justification, and reproach. For maintaining harmonious personal energy, the ideal mental state is curiosity, which supports discernment. Discernment helps us to see through confusion and encourages healing and understanding.

1: Curiosity

Curiosity promotes these goals because it is, by definition, the state of desiring to know or understand something. Curiosity also implies a kind of innocence or lack of agenda, save that of learning. The other side of discernment is judgment, and because that state fosters separation and criticism, it makes no room for curiosity. You cannot be truly curious about something while you are standing in judgment of it.

It can be hard to distinguish between curiosity and judgment by words alone. For example, the words "how can he believe that?" can have different meaning based on the energy and intent behind them. Depending on how they are said, those words can come across as either sarcastic and judgmental or as truly curious. Curious energy tries to gain information. Judgmental energy is simply expressing incredulity that anyone could possibly believe such a presumably stupid thing. Curious energy invites a harmonious flow, while judgment stops that flow. When confronted with ideas or situations that cause us to react rather than respond, we can be sure there is some judgment going on somewhere within us. Judgment, then, is a mental clue to thoughts, ideas, and their subsequent behaviors that require clearing.

We are raised in a society that values decisiveness, an ideal that was founded on Puritan principles that encourage binary thinking, particularly dividing every aspect of life into "good" and "bad." We are taught to judge: ourselves, others, ideas, cultures, foods, political ideas, anything and everything. Social media helps entrench this tendency. It gives everyone a venue to share their opinions. It encourages the tearing apart of others' opinions should they dare post anything that differs from our beliefs. Because most social media is based on short snippets, there is very little in the way of curiosity or conversation going on but rather tons of judgment, which divides and criticizes.

Until we can free ourselves from judgment, we will not make strides in understanding each other and ourselves. But it is really hard to release our almost natural inclination to judge based on what we know. To be curious is to admit that we don't know something or that we might be willing to change our opinions, and those are both unpopular ideas in our culture. We believe that we need to be decisive and strong in our beliefs and that openness to other possible opinions means we are weak. Just as emotional acceptance has a lot of cultural training working against it, mental curiosity does not find a supportive environment in our lives.

A study by Jonah Berger, a professor of social influence and author, provides a great example of how we jump to judgment based on reactions.[6] He interviewed politicians, asking them what they thought about a specific policy. When he attributed the policy

6 Shankar Vedantam, "Episode 55: Snooki and the Handbag," December 13, 2016, in *Hidden Brain*, podcast, http://www.npr.org/series/423302056/hidden -brain.

to someone from the opposing party, the politicians rejected the idea. When the same idea was presented as originating from their own party, they accepted it. There was no discernment or curiosity about the policy itself. The reaction was based solely on who was the supposed author of that idea.

We all practice this behavior to some extent. There are people, parties, and brands that we trust and ones we do not. They provide us with shortcuts to judgments and opinions. In lives as full of information and decisions as ours, these shortcuts are welcome efficiencies. However, they also subvert our curiosity and relieve us of having to practice discernment. They can make us lazy and distort our view of reality. They strip us of our freedom.

Here, though, we are speaking internal rather than external curiosity and judgment, but it works the same way. When we reflect on our own behavior or thoughts, how often do we respond, "Well, that's interesting; how can I learn more about what that means?" Instead of being curious about why we do or think what we do, we are often judgmental. The two main results of internal judgment are reproach or justification. Neither of these approaches to thinking about our actions or ideas fosters clarity, understanding, or harmony. Instead, they both, in different ways, distract us from harmony and from cultivating energy that actually serves us and our soul's purpose.

Taking Note

1. The next time you begin to react to something with judgment, stop yourself.

2. Use a clearing technique to release judgmental energy and cultivate curiosity. I suggest breath work as it is the easiest to do in the moment.

3. Instead of the judgmental comment you might have made, ask a sincerely curious question.

4. Write about the experience in your journal.

5. Repeat as necessary.

2: *Justification*

For decades now, justification has been a favored technique for allowing our inner wounded child to do whatever he or she wants. As long as we can explain away our bad behavior or poor choices, then, as they say, "it's all good"—only it isn't. Justifying is characterized by defensiveness, humor, or an almost pathological dedication to logic. Sometimes justification includes a grain of truth, something that actually explains why we are behaving the way we are. In these cases the reason is not usually because the behavior reflects our ideals.

As we know, an explanation is not an excuse and does not give us a permission slip to continue acting in ways that are against our values. And yet, it is easy and sometimes even fun to come up with complicated or off-the-wall justifications to do what our wounded self wants. When we are clever with our mental contortions, our friends laugh and praise us. When our soul gets a little too close to uncovering the root issue, our mind goes into overdrive and creates the most complex logical edifices to uphold our poor choices or bad behavior. Until we get to the core and clear the problem, justification will always win.

Justification is used for all kinds of behavior or thought patterns, but it is most useful for maintaining bad habits. Some common justifications serve behaviors like bad food choices, unhealthy addictions of all sorts, and staying in unhealthy relationships. All of these relate to our energy in three ways. First, what we take in physically affects our energy. Second, these behaviors channel our mental energy away from what we truly want in order to pacify our wounded child. Finally, they diminish our sense of self and demean our own power.

I heard somewhere that you can never win against your vices through pure willpower and that the only way to overcome them is through finding something you love more. However, the nature of justification makes that feel like a losing battle. Justifying vices creates a cushion around them. As we invest in lovingly creating the justification, we give it energy until it becomes a kind of living entity in its own right. Remember, any living thing will fight to stay alive. Emotional work is hard. Justification issues are a different kind of hard and just as insidious. For me, justification remains the most challenging aspect of personal energy work.

One of the reasons it is so tricky is because justification is a strongly woven, long-standing edifice of rationalization. When we apply curiosity to it, justification can take in curiosity and play with it like a cat with a mouse. Curiously asking "why" and "how" of an intricately devised system enlivened with its own internal logic system could keep you in an infinite loop until you exhaust yourself or find a way to break the loop. Further, we often don't question our justifications because looking too closely at how our behavior does not reflect our beliefs causes an anxiety known as cognitive dissonance.

The scary thing about justification and cognitive dissonance is that they can change who you are. The more you rationalize your behaviors, the more your mind will believe that those reasons and those behaviors become more important to you and your identity than the values you claim to hold. This is where the idea of identifying what you love more comes into play. Spending more time making yourself very clear on who you are in your heart—which is to say, the person you are in the process of becoming—is a good start to ending a cycle of justification. Instead of teasing apart justification's cat's cradle of rationalization, bypass all that and focus on the essential question: how is this behavior moving me closer to living my ideals and being free? For me, this has been the only way to successfully break this kind of behavior cycle. It is harder to find a root cause for justification of bad behavior because it is often a simple issue of the thing just feeling so good in some way, whether physically, emotionally, or psychologically. We can spend years looking for a root cause that will make ending the behavior somehow magically easier, but that is another dangerous path into the forest of justification.

Taking Note

1. What are you justifying in your life?

2. What ways have you tried to free yourself?

3. What has been most effective?

4. Beginning with an earth-based technique (see pages 57–58) can be useful to settle the mind.

5. The clearing methods that help me deal with mental justification include breath work and meditation.

6. Although mostly used as a cultivation method, consciously applied chaos can help loosen habits of justification. Changing a routine can help break up energy loops.

7. Journal about how the behavior separates you from your values. What behaviors would draw you closer to your values?

Understanding how clever our rationalizations are helps us realize how difficult this energy is to clear. By understanding, also, that it is not hiding anything worth digging for but rather is a syphon sucking away our energy, we can discover the best way to eliminate justifications. Justification can only survive if we continue to allow our energy to flow through it. The key is to focus on a behavior or behaviors that are in line with your values and consciously feed that behavior using cultivation techniques.

Deprive the justified behavior of sustenance by redirecting your energy toward what you want to thrive and toward what expresses your values. Another way to look at it is to ask what the best version of yourself would do. Choose the wolf you feed. Let the other waste away until all you have to do is clear away the dust. As with emotional clearing, it will be hard sometimes. Once something has been given life, it fights to stay alive, and starvation is a hard way to go. Justification will fight back. Just remember that letting justification starve will not kill you. In the end it will make you stronger and more authentically you. Most importantly, you will be free.

Taking Note

1. Select one of your justified behaviors (JB) that you wish to clear.

2. Refer to your initial list of values.

3. How does the JB either bring you closer to or further from your values?

4. Which value does the JB take you furthest from? (example: JB = soda addiction, value = health)

5. Create an option to choose whenever the JB wants satisfaction. (example: drink water)

6. Choose the action that supports your values and redirect your energy there.

3: Reproach

While justification allows our least awesome selves to do whatever they want and feel good about it, reproach takes us to the opposite end of the spectrum. Like most extremes, this one is just as dangerous and difficult to deal with. Who hasn't beaten themselves up over a mistake? The saying "You are your own worst critic" rings true for a reason. Sometimes we can be really great at judging others. We are masters at judging ourselves and meting out punishments worthy of far greater crimes than oversleeping, eating an extra cookie, cursing at someone while driving, or whatever it is we've done.

When we speak harshly to ourselves, for some reason it makes us feel better about the perceived or real transgression, which is really strange. On the other hand, perhaps it is not so strange. Most of our wounds were created in childhood, when we were very dependent on those around us. We had less control over our lives and were usually unable to meet our own basic needs ourselves. Mistakes that angered or upset our caregivers threatened or were perceived to threaten the meeting of our needs. Misbehaving could mean being sent to bed without dinner, which, while it might not kill us, would still feel pretty miserable, or, worse, separate us from the love and acceptance we desired from our caregivers.

These experiences might also tie into our more ancient ancestral memories in the limbic region of our brain, where mistakes were, much more often than now in the modern world, capable of killing us. Mistakes—both in our distant past and in our ancestral past—had dire consequences. Being upset because you did something that put you and perhaps others in danger seems like a normal response. The real problem for us now is that the mistakes we make, for the most part, are not life threatening. And even when a mistake is particularly dangerous—for example, cutting someone off while driving—spending time and energy in self-recrimination does not solve the problem. No amount of regretful energy will erase something. For some reason, convincing ourselves that we are unworthy of any good and decent thing in our lives seems more appropriate than analyzing what happened and either solving the problem or developing a plan so that the mistake isn't repeated.

Reproach is not simply the acknowledging of a mistake and feeling regret. Reproach is much more elaborate than that. It doesn't just make an appearance; it brings all of its luggage and moves in. Reproach is full of stories that it is happy to tell you about yourself, like how this particular mistake is a clear sign that you are a completely unworthy person who does not deserve to have any good things in their life.

When that story doesn't convince you, reproach then initiates the parade of shame, which, for me, is shown at its abhorrent best in the middle of the night. The parade of shame lines up all your mistakes, sometimes from decades ago, and forces you to feel all over again how horrible you felt at that time. Because those memories have been fed by reproach, they've grown fat and powerful and horrifying.

These are the adult version of childhood monsters hiding in the closet. If we remember just one of those nights when we have lain awake, our attention fully riveted on the parade of shame, we can see how this mental state is such a huge energy drain. Instead of getting restful sleep to refresh our body and mind, we create increasingly fretful and stagnant energy. When we rise to start the day, we are worn out and depleted. A horrible waste of our precious resources, reproach gives us nothing of value in return.

Taking Note

1. Do you have moments of reproach?

2. How about a parade of shame?

3. List some of the stories that cause reproach.

4. How have you tried to manage them?

THE POWER OF FORGIVENESS

Whether you are dealing with one reproachful situation or the whole circus, clearing this energy is, thankfully, easier than justification—*easier* but not necessarily easy, and you can probably guess why. Clearing this energy requires the strong cleansing power of forgiveness. Forgiving others is so often easier than forgiving ourselves, but just as they say you cannot love another until you love yourself, you don't truly forgive others unless you forgive yourself. Before moving on to forgiveness, make sure there isn't a learning opportunity in that memory. Ask yourself if there is a lesson you can learn from the situation. If so, note it and integrate it. If not, then you have to simply release it with self-forgiveness and grace.

Any of the clearing techniques can work, but a few that really help me in releasing reproach are breath work, tree hugging, and fire. Breath work is so easy and effective and is usually undetectable if you have to do it in public. I begin with an exhalation to expel reproach. With the inhalation, I breathe in grace. If I find myself lacking in grace, I ask the trees around (whether I can see them or not) to lend me their grace. Long, slow, deep breathing is the antidote to any kind of energy that blocks harmony and flow. After a few cycles of breath, I can feel my muscles, my blood vessels, and my soul relax and open, the reproach flushed away as grace soothes the wounds reproach left behind.

Trees are wise and wonderful beings. Sometimes it can be hard to imagine a personified deity forgiving you, especially if it resembles the Judeo-Christian god. But a tree... I've never yet thrown my arms around a tree (or, if the scene is too public, just leaned casually against a tree) and asked for help of any sort, including forgiveness, and been denied.

If my reproach parade was particularly harsh, only fire will do. Writing out all the supposed errors that render me unsuitable for anything but misery, I burn the pieces of paper. This practice is usually followed by breath work or some sort of water-based clearing.

Taking Note

1. The next time you have a reproach moment or parade of shame, select a clearing technique to release that energy.

2. Try breath work to calm your mind. Breathe out reproach; breathe in forgiveness.

3. Connect with a deity or an aspect of nature that helps you feel safe, nurtured, and loved.

4. If the reproach is persistant, consider using fire to free yourself.

5. Follow up with a cultivation practice to nourish your energy body with forgiveness and grace.

6. Gratitude can be a useful cultivation technique. Instead of reproach, view the incident through the lens of gratitude. Thank it for lessons learned and for helping develop empathy for others when they make mistakes.

REVISITING CURIOSITY

We have learned to free ourselves from the tentacles of justification and reproach, but there is still a little work to do. We must not forget that justification and reproach are the children of judgment and the opponents of curiosity. Now that we've eliminated the energy and power that justification or reproach have, we have the space to examine them and gain more information. Justification is the result when we judge something within our life to be wrong for us but prefer to indulge and create stories as to why it is okay (ironically, justification is usually right—the behavior is often out of line with our values). Turning the judgment of justification into discernment, we can consciously say that "this behavior is not in line with my values." Then we can acknowledge that we want to do it anyway.

Now we bring in curiosity. Instead of judging ourselves, we explore. We ask ourselves why we want to do that thing. We ask without trying to prove that it is okay, which is falling back into justification. The answers could be anything from "It's my pacifier" to "Well, I can't just be a doormat and let them walk all over me." These answers lead to more questions, such as "Why do I need pacifying?" or "Is this behavior stopping people from walking all over me?" By being curious and digging deeply, you can discover hidden areas that you can clear. If something in your life is so hard to bear that you require pacification, then by attending to it energetically, you can really free yourself.

Once the grasp of reproach has been loosened, your curious heart can discover what can be learned from that experience. Usually a clear-headed examination of the experience will reveal that a simple fix will keep the situation from reoccurring: creating a better organizational system so things are not forgotten, apologizing to someone, removing distractions from your car so you

can focus on your driving. Most of the things we reproach ourselves for are so small that when we step back, we wonder why
we worked ourselves up over it. That's a good thing to wonder
about. It is usually because we have been trained to harshly judge
ourselves and others. We have been taught that one mistake can
tarnish an otherwise lovely character. We have come to believe
that an outward show of remorse equals true repentance. This,
though, is similar to emotional indulgence. Dramatic expressions
are not as powerful as changed behavior.

It might seem confusing that I suggest eliminating justification and reproach before looking at what is underneath, which
is the process we took with the emotional clues. Based on my
experience, our minds are so powerful that it seems impossible to
get close to anything underneath justification or reproach until we
clear away some of that energy. Justification and reproach seem to
take any energy thrown at it, eat it up, and grow stronger. That's
why I think they are more like energy siphons or channels for
energy rather than simply energy. Loosen their grip, weaken their
strength through starvation and forgiveness, and it will be easier
to see if anything of value remains.

YOU HAVE THE KEYS
TO YOUR SHADOW CLOSET

The truth is that you do deserve good things in your life. In fact,
you deserve the very best thing in life: to be the person you were
born to be. It is not just a selfish goal, either. Remember that the
person that you were born to be brings important medicine to the
world. You have something of great value, and you have a responsibility to honor that gift by bestowing it upon and expressing it in
the world. Now you have some great tools to help you do that. You
can recognize behavior patterns that are incongruent with your

core values as clues to stagnant energy or energy siphons that are inappropriately controlling your life. You have some understanding of how the energy resulting from traumas hides essential parts of you in your shadow closet. You know that the items in your shadow closet are far more complex and valuable than you first imagined. You even have the steps for freeing those precious gifts:

1. Identify a behavior pattern by paying attention to
   - cyclical behaviors;
   - disproportionate emotional responses; and
   - behavior that does not reflect your values.

2. Clear anxiety with a simple clearing technique such as breath work, mountain pose, washing your hands, holding a crystal, or smelling an essential oil. As you work with various techniques, you'll learn which ones are effective for you.

3. Observe and identify:
   - Are you reacting or responding?
   - Where is the behavior located: mental or emotional energy body?
   - What is really going on underneath the behavior pattern?

4. Look for underlying patterns that point to deeper roots.

These steps are just the beginning. Practice them so that observing yourself becomes second nature. Once you read the next chapter, you will be able to fully identify the hidden gift, integrate it, and clear away any residual energy. But before we develop a plan for addressing trouble areas, we'll work on integrating basic healthy energy hygiene practices into your current life.

CHAPTER 8

YOUR PERSONAL ENERGY PRACTICE

One of the keys for developing a healthy energy practice is to work small actions into your current life. Because we are all so busy and because developing new habits can be challenging, the more effortlessly integrated the practice, the more likely you are to maintain it. With a little creativity, it is easy to slip small efforts into the already existing habits and routines of your day. Beginning with smaller actions, we can prepare ourselves for the more intricate work of deep energy clearing.

Working on the deeper issues discussed in the previous chapters requires more time and attention. This work is easier and more productive when you start from a place of relative stability. Considering the body as a metaphor, if someone needs major surgery, healthcare providers make sure the patient is stable before attempting that procedure, when possible, to insure the best chance of success and recovery. A body that is malnourished or battered cannot begin muscle building until its basic needs are met. In addition, after a period of basic energy maintenance, it is easier to identify how harmonious energy feels.

I suggest that you begin incorporating basic energetic practices into your daily life while continuing to note moments when your behavior does not match your ideals or when you are reacting rather than responding to situations. Notice them, clear the immediate anxiety, and track them in a planner or journal. We'll use that information as we begin the serious work of freeing yourself and moving toward energetic harmony.

BUILDING HABITS

Just as it is easier to clean and organize a closet by first emptying it, we will spend time on clearing. Once we create some space within our energy body, we will feel more comfortable and be able to see ourselves more clearly. After clearing, you may feel like a weight has been lifted, your throat has opened up, or tight ropes that bound you are suddenly released. A really visceral example for me is that a good clearing feels like I just took off a pair of shoes that were too tight.

You will probably use a wider variety of clearing techniques throughout your day than containing or cultivating, at least in the beginning. Eventually the ratio will shift to cultivation because once you've cleared as much as you can and have developed daily clearing habits, you'll have more space to cultivate the energy you desire and require less clearing. Containing, which in itself is a stabilizing practice, will remain mostly constant unless you find yourself occasionally in circumstances that require, for example, more protection than your regular daily life.

To begin creating phase one of your personal practice, review the clearing techniques in chapter 3 and your notes from your journal. Pick at least three of the techniques that worked for you. Now think about your daily life and the things you do on a routine basis, such as brushing your teeth, showering, having that first cup of coffee or maybe preparing a smoothie, taking a walk, driving to work, or even journaling, exercising, meditating, or doing yoga. It doesn't matter what the activities are as long as you do them every day or at least five times a week regularly. Weekends are sometimes less structured, and that's okay. With these kinds of practices, daily is great, but five days a week is better than zero days a week.

Now match up three of the clearing techniques on your list with three activities. Combine a technique with an already established daily practice that makes sense. For example, if you take a daily walk or do any sort of physical movement, you can make it do double duty by coupling the activity with intention, mindfulness, and attention. Here are some examples:

- As you brush your teeth daily, you can finish up by gargling to clear your throat of stagnant energy that may color your tone of voice with annoyance, impatience, or anger. Combining a technique with teeth brushing is a good choice because almost all of us do that at least once a day.

- When you wash your hands, focus on inappropriate energy flowing from throughout your body to your hands and down the drain.

- You can stand in mountain pose while you brush your hair or teeth, grounding any inappropriate or stagnant energy into the earth.

- If you drive somewhere every day, you have a great opportunity to incorporate breath work.

Be creative and look for opportunities to blend energy practices into your already existing routine.

There will be times when you will employ a technique on an "as needed" basis. That's part of the beauty of energy work: you can call on these skills whenever and wherever necessary. Having a handful of small practices that you do every day will establish two important things. First, you will gain mastery and confidence so that you can recall a technique like a muscle memory. Second, you will learn through experience which ones work best for you in certain circumstances. If remembering three new things each day is challenging, make notes for yourself and leave them in the area where the activity takes place and in a way that causes you to actually touch the note. For example, you can put a sticky note on your toothpaste so you touch the note when you pick up the tube; put a note on your gearshift in your car; or roll up a note and stick it in your walking shoe so you have to remove it each day when you walk.

I can't say it enough: be creative. And be proactive. This is your life and your energy—and don't forget you have good brains. However, if three things really are too much, and you know yourself well enough to know if this is the case, try two or even just one. It is far better to do one thing for a month, discover you love the benefits, and therefore become more motivated to add another. You will find yourself getting hungry for harmonious energy, so even if you start really small, you will experience a cumulative effect. It can be hard to identify the line between being lazy and being cruel to yourself. Hold yourself accountable, but do not fall into beating yourself up.

After a few weeks, assess how your practices are working. By working, I don't mean to measure the change in your energy, although you should definitely be noticing differences already. More importantly, are you finding that the practices feel natural in the rhythm of your life? Is it easy to slip them in without stress? Are you enjoying them at all? If not, consider trying new ones. Altering a plan is not failure; it is part of the process. You are the best judge of your life and can determine for yourself if the efforts and results work for you. If your routine needs tweaking, spend some time doing that and repeat as necessary. I wouldn't move on to cultivation until you establish your clearing practices because it is not as useful to cultivate if there is no space.

ADDING CONTAINMENT
& CULTIVATION SKILLS

Now that you've cleared some energy, you have space to cultivate. But first we will contain all that nice clean space you've created. I suggest starting with just one containing technique. Containing doesn't have to happen every day, although there is nothing wrong with a daily routine. Once a week would be just fine. To make things as effortless as possible, try to select one that can build on to one of the clearing techniques you've established. For example, if you are doing breath work in your car each day, you can easily incorporate the bubble of light technique directly following that. Cording works well in conjunction with taking a shower or even undressing each night for bed. Namaste hands are built right in to yoga, so if you do that with intention, you're good to go.

When you are ready to incorporate cultivation techniques, tread carefully. It is tempting to want to fill up the space you are creating with new energy. Moving too fast will not give you the time you need to make sure the practices are bringing in the energy you intended and to determine if that energy feels right. I would also not recommend bringing consciously applied chaos at this point, although if it seems appropriate, then by all means give it a go. However, I would try to select one of the other techniques and start small. For example, intentional consumerism is a huge category. It would be overwhelming to try and change all your consuming habits. Instead, just pick one thing to focus on at a time.

Maybe you will cull your social media to eliminate sources that don't provide information that feeds your soul and seek out more that do. Perhaps you will decide that it is time to divest your living space of items that don't serve a purpose or add value to your life. Maybe the idea of spending a few minutes in grateful prayer each night appeals to you. My best suggestions are breath work, gratitude, or prayer/contemplation. If you want a more active technique, pick an area that is cluttered and used on a regular basis, such as your sock drawer, bathroom counter, or desk. Clear it and keep it clear, as well as take good care of all the items in that area. The guidance I can provide for cultivation is limited because once you've begun clearing and containing, you will develop a sense for what will best serve you. Cultivation is so personal because everyone is different and everyone's lives are different. While it is easy enough to share common techniques in clearing the stagnant or inappropriate energy that we all experience, the type of energy we wish to cultivate can vary so much from person to person.

It is good to remember, too, that the perfect recipe for energetic harmony will change as we move through our lives. Just as our bodies' needs change, so do our energetic needs. As you progress in your practice, pay attention to how things feel, both in terms of the practices you've adopted and the energy shifts within yourself. Because you are still developing an understanding of your energy body, at first you might not notice the subtle shifts in energetic needs from day to day, but if you do, don't be alarmed. That is good. It means you are acquiring awareness of and sensitivity to your energetic harmony. As time goes on, you will become more sensitive to shifts in your energy and be able to address those changes right away, eliminating any potential larger or long-term issues. Don't forget to continue tracking your moments of when your behavior doesn't match your ideals. We'll use that data starting in the next phase.

DEEP CLEARING

Now that you have established some routines for yourself and experienced how it feels to release stagnant and inappropriate energy and to create vibrant energy with specific characteristics, we can move on to addressing some of the larger issues that keep us from living freely. Of course we will all have unique concerns, traumas, wounds, triggers, and biases, but we can identify some general principles to apply to most situations. There is no ideal schedule, just guidelines to employ only if they are useful. The most important thing is that your initial basic energy practice feels stable and effective to you before moving on. Take as much time as you need.

It is highly advisable to start with only one major block at a time. Because you have been keeping track of occurrences for a while, you have an idea about which types are most prevalent or controlling in your life. Selecting the biggest, most powerful block is tempting, but resist that temptation. Start with a smaller one. Think of this as training wheels. You're more likely to be successful in the long run if you experience success early on. This initial dive into deep closet cleaning will have a large learning curve. The experience you gain will help so much as you move forward. If the task feels too large or like there is too much at stake, it will add a layer of anxiety that you don't need. However, if you are motivated by challenge, then ignore my suggestion and do what will work best for you.

Just as all our shadow closet issues will be different, so will our experiences in dealing with them. So far none of my interactions with my shadow closet has been the same. I attribute this to the important role the soul plays in this work. The soul is where the fertile soil of future growth is created using all the fragments of ourselves that we release; in other words, the parts that we deem as garbage and add to the compost pile (see appendix B for a little more information on this idea). The soul doesn't necessarily work according to the conscious mind's timeline.

There will be points in the process where it feels like nothing is happening. Sometimes there is nothing you can do except wait patiently for the soul to reveal its secrets to your consciousness. This is so frustrating because we want to do something—to work at the problem and be proactive—and this is part of our challenge as the people of Western civilization. All you can do is continue on with your daily energy work and trust the process. It'll be worth it in the end, I promise. As you continue to cultivate the kind of energy that will, for you, promote understanding, reflection, and insight, the information that you seek will be revealed. Your soul will have taken in everything that you provide and turned it into a pearl of wisdom. Keep in mind that this is a very organic process and that you are an organic being with various aspects existing together. Each aspect has its own nature, including its own sense of time. In the meantime, we'll do what we can to help the conscious mind do what it can to support the process. We will do this by following a few simple steps, beginning with noticing behaviors that do not reflect our beliefs and clearing the anxious energy that often comes with these moments. Then, so we can deal with it appropriately, we will explore what is really going on to discover whether it is an emotional block or a mental misdirection.

Notice

As has been mentioned a few times, the first step is to notice occurrences of behavior that are not in line with your values. One clue is feeling anxiety, shame, or fear in addition to whatever other feelings are going on. You may feel a lack of control as well. This is huge because in order to live as free beings, we must be in control of ourselves. If we are not in control, then we are being controlled by something else, which is the opposite of freedom.

Clear

When you notice the behavior, clear the anxious or shameful energy around it using any simple clearing technique (breath work or walking work well for me). You won't be able to objectively examine the experience while filled with anxiety, fear, or shame.

It may be that this is all you can do in the moment, especially if you are interacting with someone, and that's okay. You can finish the process when you have appropriate privacy. I would strongly suggest, though, that you let your loved ones know that you are working on some issues and might at times ask to stop an interaction in the middle of it in order to do this work. Being that they are your loved ones and want you to be as happy and healthy as possible, hopefully they will be understanding and supportive. While you can certainly continue working on blocks after the fact, there is something valuable about being able to examine the experience in the moment.

Explore

When you can, either after the fact or by taking a break in the moment, explore the nature of the block. Are you repressing or indulging emotionally? Are you justifying or reproaching? Are you fancy and doing a complex combo deal? Identify as much detail as possible about what you are experiencing and doing. Include information such as in what way the behavior is reactive rather than responsive. How does it widen the gap between your current self and the person you want to be? If you were truly living your beliefs in this moment, what would that look like? If you have been gathering data over the past few months about other occurrences, compare what you've collected with the present situation. Look for any type of similarities: emotions, actions, triggering events, locations, other people. This isn't essential, but being able to see larger patterns is always helpful, if for no other reason than to show you how many ways you are being controlled by missing parts of yourself or by energetic misdirection.

Identify

If the block is emotional and therefore associated with your shadow closet, the information from multiple occurrences can be really useful. The data can make it easier to see the story that you are connecting to the emotional reaction. This is the next step: identifying the story attached to the behavior. Remember that the story is not the treasure but rather a clue that points to the treasure. This is a part of the process that can take time. Sometimes we don't remember things because we don't want to. We are protecting ourselves from traumatic experience. Ironically, that does not save us from reliving that trauma over and over again because the wound is not healed. Only by remembering can we fully release it and never have to relive it again. Equally as important, we will also reclaim a part of ourselves that was locked away.

To help the mind and the soul reveal this necessary information more readily, combine a clearing technique (a shower or bath is ideal) with a cultivation technique. Cultivate a safe space conducive to calmly uncovering your secrets. I think the cultivation technique that works best for this is prayer or meditation. Within the sacred space of intimacy with the Divine or your highest self, request help in letting your heart and emotional energy body know that the past is in the past and can no longer cause pain. Ask to be reminded that you actually already lived through it and the worst did not happen; you did not die. Ask that your mind and your soul work together to bring the memory of the initial instance to your consciousness.

As you wait for this information to be revealed, continue stopping yourself when you repeat the behavior, clearing the anxiety, and trying to shift from reaction to response through your will. To support this, cultivate energy that feeds your will and your desire to release this block. This creates a two-pronged approach encouraging both your conscious and unconscious to work toward the same goal. When both paths meet, the remaining energy can be cleared. Follow this with a containment practice, and continue with your cultivation work as long as is necessary.

Mental versus Emotional

If the block—or, more precisely, misdirection—is mental, the process is different and in some ways easier but in other ways more challenging. For example, with emotional issues the conscious mind sometimes has to wait on the unconscious mind and the soul. This can be frustrating, especially for those who like to keep to a timetable and track progress (I happen to be one of these types). Mental issues are more within your conscious control, which brings us to the way these blocks are more challenging. With emotional blocks, there is always something below the surface. Bringing it up is the hard part, but once it is revealed, things usually fall into place really quickly and seem so obvious that it is almost like magic. With justification and reproach, there is no cavalry that will ride up from the depths to save the day. You are in control and that's comforting, as you can control the timeline, though it leaves much of the responsibility on your will. Whether you are feeding a different wolf in order to starve out a justification or pouring the grace of forgiveness over your mistakes, these are choices you make in real time and actions that you deliberately take.

After you have cleared your first deep block and enjoyed the relief and joy of having either reclaimed a part of yourself or cut off an energy syphon, you will want to continue removing more blocks. You may wish to clear whatever is most limiting your freedom, and you are now well prepared to do so. Or you may decide to let the issues arise in your consciousness more organically. Once you become accustomed to noticing behaviors that are out of line with your beliefs, you will notice more and more. That may sound awful to think about, but it really isn't because rather than becoming a parade of shame, it becomes a bunch of opportunities to embrace freedom. The longer I do this work, something else I've noticed is that at some point I don't think about "doing the work." It has, instead, become the way I live my life. I notice a problem; I deal with it. The process flows easily and organically, with less stress and internal conflict.

THE CLEAR ENERGY LIFESTYLE

Once you have established an initial energy practice and developed a knack for deep cleansing for repetitive issues, you can begin to relax into your new life. Just as cultivating good physical health requires a change in habits, so does cultivating harmonious energetic health. You have actually already done this. Simply keep up with your practices and continue dealing with the larger issues one at a time.

With experience, you will develop techniques that you need only in specific situations. You will notice that when there are changes in your life, you might reconsider your everyday practices to make sure they are still most appropriate. Also, as you change, which you will as you continue to reclaim parts of yourself, you will find your practices changing. The freer you are and the less controlled by external circumstances, the larger your comfort zone will be. When your comfort zone is robust, you will be less easily thrown off-course—and, conversely, you will notice more quickly when something is off, and you can then calmly and confidently deal with it.

Sample Personal Energy Practice

This is based largely on my current practice. However, by the time this is published, it will likely have changed. Remember that as we evolve and our environments change, so will our practices. Also note that this does not include the energy work I do for my home. That will be included in the next chapter.

DAILY

- morning coffee and reflection
- morning walk and grounding
- evening prayer and blessing (see chapter 10 for more on blessings)
- as needed: breath work, washing hands, intentional consumerism

WEEKLY

- email and desktop clearing
- yin yoga

MONTHLY

- decording
- declutter something

ONGOING

- tracking and clearing emotional reactions and mental judgments

CONSEQUENCES

This work, this attending to our energy body and freeing our whole selves, is amazing. You are already awesome; you know that. But some of that awesome is hidden or starved due to emotional or mental energy issues. As you embrace more freedom, your world will open up. Possibilities that never occurred to you before will not only seem possible but probable. Dreams that you thought were most dear to you may fall away, making space for bigger dreams that feel closer and more real than the old ones ever did. You will change. You may change in ways that you don't expect. Always trust the process. Always know that as you become more whole, you only become better and more able to fully express your soul's purpose in the world.

The people around you may not always appreciate the changes, especially if they themselves are in a state of reaction controlled by emotional or mental blocks. This is not surprising. We've all seen it in our lives. Whenever we or someone else around us changes, there are consequences that ripple out from the changed person, affecting others in his or her life. Try to remember that they are scared, even if they are acting angry or mean (perhaps especially if). You will want to handle the people in your life in ways that reflect your core values and highest ideals. It might not always be easy, and it might require a little distance before reconnecting and healing. Even though it might be scary because you could lose someone from your life, at least in the short term, please do not give up becoming the person you were meant to be. Your journey will take you wherever you should go and surround you with the people you need. It can be such a challenging situation, as you have to always make sure you are leaning toward discernment and not judgment.

After you've established some stability in your own energy body, once you have actively participated in the co-creation of yourself, which is really the freeing of yourself, you can turn those skills to the space around you, the energy that extends beyond your energy body and even toward others. As you continue to craft your whole and free self, you get to consciously participate in the co-creation of the world. Sound exciting? Then read on, my friend.

PART 3

YOUR ENVIRONMENT

Everything and everyone is connected. We understand this idea, but we also accept that we are separate, unique beings. Reality is, apparently, made of mystery and the tension between two opposing ideas. This may be why life is endlessly fascinating. As we expand our skills in energy management, we realize this contradiction more fully. We are individuals responsible for our own energy bodies. We also know that our energy affects the world around us, just as our environment affects us. As your abilities grow, the line between you and not-you is stretched thinner and thinner. This realization opens up amazing possibilities and brings with it serious responsibility. After all, you are not only taking good care of yourself, you are creating the world.

Before we get into manifesting changes that affect the planet, we'll start smaller. Specifically, we'll talk about making sure the spaces you inhabit most frequently are energetically supporting your goals and values. This part, I think, is what most people are interested in. It can be a lot of fun and has plenty of room for creativity. After the hard work of taking care of our personal energy bodies, this will seem so much easier. Part of the reason is that there will be a smaller learning curve because so much of the knowledge and skills you gained in the previous section translate very easily to this section.

CHAPTER 9

YOUR PERSONAL SPACE

Whether you are a homebody who works from a home office, an itinerant world traveller who works from anywhere on the globe, or a person who divides your time between home, school, work, and car, you have a sphere of influence. For those just learning to control and manage energy, that sphere is probably smaller than that of someone who has been practicing for a while. As your skill and confidence grow, so can your sphere of influence. The extent to which you can influence any space depends not only on you and your practice but also on the energy of those with whom you share your space, as well as any spirits of the buildings or land who also reside or happen to be in that space. It is a two-way street. Your sphere influences the world around you, and you are, in turn, influenced by external energy.

This symbiotic relationship means that, depending on the strength and will of the other energies involved, you will probably not be able to simply impose your desires entirely on the space in question. However, you can use what you know to nurture the energy that best reflects your values. Perhaps you will find that your energy work influences those around you in ways that benefit them, so everyone wins. This last idea is really exciting and will be explored more thoroughly in the next chapter.

Instead of always saying "your home, your office, your car, etc.," which can get really cumbersome, we will just refer to "the space," knowing that it refers to whatever space you happen to be working with. We can do this because the principles remain the same, no matter what kind of area we are talking about. Of course, some of the techniques will not be possible in all types of spaces. It is not likely, for example, that you can burn sage in your office or cubical or at your cash register. You can, though, use other methods that are just as effective. I'll leave it to you, your common sense, and your knowledge of your own circumstances to determine what is most appropriate from the options discussed. With energy work, there are always options.

CARING FOR THE ENERGY OF A SPACE

You will probably not be surprised to know that you can use most of the same techniques to clear a space as you do to clear your own energy. In fact, you are likely already a few steps ahead of me and realize that some of the techniques you've used have already affected the energy of your space. For example, if you've begun clearing your desk and desktop as a way of clearing your own mental clutter, you have probably noticed that the energy in your work area also feels smoother and more peaceful. Or perhaps you've begun being very mindful of the physical things you own and how you care for them. That relationship that you've fostered and made healthy has already begun radiating from you and the items in question to the space that contains them. As above, so below; as below, so above…and everything is connected.

If you have done any kind of personal clearing work that involves your belongings or your space, you likely have also developed sensitivity to energy in general. You might notice how the energy of a space changes when you do a particular action, or perhaps you notice the change in energy as you move from part of your workplace to another. Just by paying attention, you learn to sense what is difficult to put into words. The more you live this way, the more nuanced your recognition and understanding of different kinds of energy become.

What if you don't feel energy the way you imagine someone else does? What if you walk around all day and only feel what you consider to be obvious energy, but you feel like you are deaf and blind to more subtle changes or shifts? Please do not worry about that. This is metaphysical energy we are dealing with. There is no absolute way to register and measure it. Also, keep in mind that there are lots of different ways of knowing. You may not have a physical sensation. For example, in intuitive and psychic work, people talk about clairvoyance, which is literally "clear seeing." The clairvoyant person sees images and interprets those images into messages. There are other "clairs" as well. Clairsentience is "clear sensing," or someone who feels or senses information, often in a physical way. I think many people think that clairsentience is the only or best way to sense energy, but it is not the only way. Clairaudient people hear information. These are the most commonly discussed.

As a tarot reader, I was always dismayed that I never seemed to have any skill in these clairs. It wasn't until years into my study that I learned about another clair: claircognizance. Claircognizance is "clear knowing" and means that you do not have a physical sensation such as seeing, feeling, or hearing, but rather you just know something. Apparently this was my special skill—one that I don't always appreciate because the "knowing" comes as thoughts, and it can be really challenging to know which thought is simply my own or one that comes from somewhere external. When I talk to other people with other skills, though, I find that everyone has the same concerns. Sure, someone may "hear" something, but they don't always know if what they heard was internally or externally generated.

The point is that you should not berate or doubt yourself because you think you aren't feeling energy properly or clearly. Trust me, if you've been doing your personal energy management, you have enough self-awareness and understanding to work with external energy. As you continue on, you will learn to trust yourself and your experiences. Furthermore, you do not always have to feel a specific energy to clear it. There are other ways to tell if an inappropriate energy is present. In fact, the best and most reliable way is to know how things feel when they are in harmony. If you know what your home feels like when it is in energetic harmony, then you will know when it is not in harmony. Unlike personal energy bodywork, you don't have to identify the nature of the block and trace it to a root cause. You can simply do a general clearing to remove the inappropriate, usually stagnant, energy.

I should point out that this is true for most places and in most circumstances. While there are more troublesome energy situations, such as ghosts or bitter land spirits (they usually have good reason for being bitter), those are not as common in everyday life as we might imagine. In those cases, it is best to call in a specialist. We don't need to deal with those sorts of varsity-level cases in our daily lives. For the most part, you are completely capable of taking care of your own spaces, just as you are able to care for your own energy body.

Even if you think you aren't skilled at sensing energy, you picked up this book for a reason, and that reason probably had to do with feeling like something is feeling off. That alone shows that you are capable of sensing energy. Armed with the knowledge you gained from managing your personal energy, you are ready to cultivate healthy energy all around you. Once you are moving toward energetic harmony and living your values, it becomes easier to notice when the space around you is in disharmony. As a being with free will and the power to co-create with the universe, you have the opportunity and means to help the world around you find and maintain harmony.

In general terms, we know the purposes, if you will, of spaces. They are created for reasons. Homes are created to provide safe and comfortable places for people to live, to find peace and restoration, to create, and to love each other. Cars are meant to transport people safely from place to place. Ideally, workspaces are dedicated to foster a convenient and productive environment where people can do good work. I know, sometimes it doesn't feel that way, but if your workplace isn't in energetic harmony, you can help change that. Even the work you've already done for yourself will begin changing the energy at work because if you are living your values, even if others are not, you cannot help but affect change. Your harmonious energy, which will be manifested through your actions and behavior, will ripple outward, like a stone thrown in a pond. Just as you helped yourself move into closer alignment with your values and life's purpose, you can help spaces move toward fulfilling their purpose.

Now that you have experience clearing your own energy, you will find clearing spaces to be really easy. Honestly, clearing our internal mental and emotional energy is probably some of the hardest work we will do in our lives. Most books or learning curves start easy and get harder or more complex as you go deeper, but the opposite is true here.

This may sound like a silly metaphor, but maybe it will make sense for you. When I was younger and really interested in cosmetics, and home parties were all the rage, I remember the presenters at these gatherings always started with skin care: cleansing, conditioning, and special treatments. They never wanted to sell you the fun stuff—lipstick, eye shadow, mascara, etc.—until after your skin was in good shape. They said that you needed a healthy foundation first before adding the fun touches of color.

Energy work is like that. You have to be strong, clear, and centered within your own energy body before you can do the more outwardly dramatic stuff. The cosmetics people were right, though. No matter how much color you add to your face, it is no substitute for the health of your skin. Likewise, you can clear a space twice a day, but if you are an energetic mess, it won't matter. Your energetic disharmony will contaminate the space. It'll only be a temporary fix. That said, you don't have to be "perfect" at all or all the time to take care of the space around you. We are always works in progress. Moving toward health and harmony, though, is different from repeating the same cycles of disharmony.

One thing to keep in mind is that you are the most important aspect to any further energy work you want to do. Part of you and your energy is your will. The ideas and processes that I share below form a template that you can use to create your own unique practice. Whatever you do, it should originate from your center, your beliefs, your values. Some of you will have challenging circumstances, such as space shared with unsympathetic individuals or a workplace with privacy or other issues, so some of my ideas will not apply. I've tried to include alternatives, but you are a creative being and can devise solutions to any problem. Where there is a will, there is a way. If you have the will to care for the energy of a space, no matter the situation, you will create a way to do so.

In my belief system, everything, including energy, is connected, not just to everything else but also to the Divine. My sense of the Divine is that it is not rigid, demanding very particular and specific ritualistic actions. Instead, it is fluid, with a tendency toward harmony. It is willing to work with you. Be open, be creative, and be responsible.

The process described below is a basic clearing, containment, and cultivation method that I use both for places that I'm asked to clear and for my own home, which I do once a month as regular care and also as needed. If I am having people over, for example, I will do this as well. You will see that you can customize this, particularly the cultivation aspect, to create an energetic space that supports exactly what you want. After that, we'll focus on tips for ongoing energy work within a space and portable energy tools for keeping other things (car, luggage, etc.) energetically harmonious and safe.

BASIC SPACE CLEARING, CONTAINMENT, AND CULTIVATION

Clearing

For a space that is new to you or for the first time you clear a space, even if you are otherwise familiar with it, take the time to get acquainted with it as it is before doing anything. Start at one point and walk around the whole parameter, circling in to follow the parameters of each wall of each room, opening doors to closets, opening shower curtains, getting as close to the corners as possible, and checking behind doors that are usually open against a wall. I do not open all the cupboards and drawers, but you can if you want, particularly if they don't get opened very often.

Focus on two things during this initial walk: getting acquainted with the space and paying attention to any blatantly "off" energy. If you feel like there is something larger or more disharmonious than you think you want to tackle, consider calling in a professional or even a friend with more experience. In general, you can expect to find a combination of energy that basically feels appropriate or harmonious with pockets of stagnation. After you have cleared a space once, you probably don't have to do this slow, investigative, exploratory initial walk through again. I try to keep things as simple as possible because then I'm more likely to do the work. But for the first time, it is worth the time investment, both so you can get used to walking methodically around the space paying attention to nothing but the energy and to become familiar with that specific space.

Shake and Wake

Clearing energy in a space can be done any number of ways but I find a two-step clearing process to work best for me. The first part is breaking up and waking up the energy. Stagnant energy needs to be broken up or shaken up to make removal easier. Appropriate energy likes to be woken up from time to time to keep it from becoming stagnant. Remember energy is meant to flow. To break and shake energy, I prefer noise and use a hand bell. If you don't have a bell, you can clap, bang a spoon on a pan, or fill a small container with dried beans and shake it. You don't have to buy anything. For spaces where noise would be inappropriate, such as in a shared office space, you can use air to move the energy either by blowing or using a handheld fan. You could even unobtrusively wave your hand.

Decide on the noisemaker or energy moving technique you are going to use and pick the starting point. For a space with multiple floors, I start from the top floor and work my way down. For clearing, I move counterclockwise. That is not necessary at all, especially if it has no meaning to you. My reasoning comes from my magical training, which uses widdershins (or counterclockwise movement) for releasing energy. If that makes sense for you, even if it isn't part of your current belief system, do incorporate it. Anything that you imbue with symbolic meaning will strengthen your work. As above, so below.

Move through space, following the walls, give extra attention to corners, closets, and areas behind doors or furniture. Go at a moderate pace. Don't move so slowly that the process takes too long (you'll be walking this route several more times!) but go slowly enough that you can sense any particularly stubborn areas of stagnation. If you do, stop and rattle or bang or clap until you feel like the energy has loosened.

I usually talk to the energy as I do this. If I had any musical sense or rhythm, I would probably have a nice chant that I could use each time. Instead, I talk to it the way I talk to my dog when no one is around. I'm sure some of you know what I mean. I say things like, "Okay, guys, it's time to wake up! Let's shake it up and shake it out. Look lively. No more snoozing. That means you, hiding in the corner. I have my eye on you." You should not copy what anyone else says but instead, just be natural, be yourself. You are developing a relationship with this space, with energy in general. Don't begin that relationship by being someone you aren't. I'm kind of casual and sometimes I think I'm funny, so that's how I talk to energy. Use your voice and words to convey the idea of waking up and shaking off the dust of inertia. Again, if you are working in a public space where you cannot use your voice, say the words in your head. This works, just make sure your focus is laser sharp. Do this all through the space.

Cleansing

Head back to your starting point for phase two of clearing: cleansing. This is the phase where we actively release any inappropriate or stagnated energy. If you've been dying to use your sage stick, now is the time to break it out, although you can use any other cleansing technique that you prefer. Any type of incense that you associate with cleansing is appropriate. Solar- or gem-infused water can be sprayed or sprinkled as a cleansing agent. Walking through with a candle (or a flashlight if candle fumes or smoke irritates you) works, too. Using the flashlight on your smart phone can be a quiet, subtle method for public places.

If you are using a sage bundle, I have some tips. You burn the sage bundle the same as you would a stick incense. Light a small portion, let it burn for a moment, then blow it out. It should still smolder even though it is not actually on fire. If it is tightly bundled, carry your lighter (a long handled one is easiest) with you in case it goes out. If it does, simply relight it, perhaps blowing gently on the glowing part to keep it active. If you have a loose bundle, carry a plate or other fire resistant receptacle to catch the ashes, as there will be more than with a tight bundle.

For water, use a dedicated spray bottle, especially if you add essential oils. If you don't have a spray bottle or don't want to spray the water, simply have the water in a mug with a handle, to make it easier to carry with one hand, using the other to disperse the water. Dip a few fingers in and flick to spread the water. You don't need to douse the space; just a light, symbolic application is fine. When working with a candle, place it in a safe holder with a base wide enough to catch any drips.

Retrace your route from the shake and wake step, going in the same direction. Make sure the smoke, water, or light is directed through the whole space, paying attention to the same hiding places for stagnant energy (corners, behind doors, etc.). Again, talk to the energy, telling it what you want it to do. You can develop your own set phrases or chants, or just chat with it as I do. I say things like, "Any inappropriate or stagnant energy, go back to the earth to be redistributed to your rightful place" and, because I crack myself up, "You don't have to go home, but you can't stay here!" But I let it know I'm joking because it really does have to go home.

When you are done, blow out the candle if you used one. If you are using a sage stick, you can dip it in water quickly, just enough to put it out but not soak the whole bundle. I have a cauldron filled with sand and put my sage bundle, lit side down, into the sand. One of my teachers said that if you use sage, when you are done, you must let any remaining sage burn until it is all gone as an offering. I do not do that. My current sage bundle is thickly and tightly woven, a long-lasting tool. That sage bundle and I have formed a relationship. I always thank my tools but don't feel the need to sacrifice them after each use.

Containment

That is all it takes to clear a space, but we don't stop there. Once your space is nice and clean, you want to do what you can to keep it that way. In other words, you want to contain and protect the energy. Because I like to keep things simple and efficient, I set up a containment network. That's not as high-tech or complicated as it might sound. Once a year, I sprinkle salt around the outside perimeter of my property and put acorns in my windowsills (each fall I gather new acorns). Before sprinkling the salt or placing the acorns, I bless and charm them with the job of protecting and containing the energy of the home by asking them to only allow in energy that is beneficial and appropriate. You could use runes, crystals, or any stones that have a protective energy to you. As you can tell, I like earthy things for containment, but don't be afraid to be creative and use what is meaningful to you.

When you have the containment laid out, the next time you do this work (I do mine once per month), you don't have to walk the outside property line again. You can stand in the center of the space, or if you are in a home and have a room or space where you usually do magical or spiritual work, you can stand there. Stand strongly, grounded and centered, like in mountain pose. Using your breath, deeply inhale the strong, protective energy of the earth. Exhale, pushing that energy to the edges of your space, touching and strengthening your salt, acorns, runes, or stones. Visualize your space's energetic boundary, seeing it strong and vibrant. I often also visualize a wall of fire that rises up from the boundary, burning away any stagnant energy and purifying any areas that need a boost.

Cultivation

This is the last step and the one where you get to imbue your space with precisely the kind of energy you want. Creating a space that supports you in living your values is so helpful. While we can live according to our ideals in any situation, no matter how dire or difficult, it is easier to do so in a supportive environment. For this part I use a rattle, one that is dedicated to blessing work. You can use a rattle that is specially made or even a container with dried beans or rice in it. A spray bottle with rose or lavender water is nice, too. As with cleansing, incense that is associated with the energy you want to cultivate will work, as will using a candle or a light.

Before starting (you'll be following your same route one more time), take the time to identify exactly what energy you want to invite. It can be the same every time or it can vary. My list varies depending on what is going on in my life (or work, since I work from home). I try to keep it to five types so I don't forget or get mixed up. For example, let's say we want to invite peace, love, creativity, and abundance. This time I walk clockwise because in my tradition that is the direction to raise energy, but again, use what is meaningful to you, although I'd suggest going in the opposite direction as you did for the clearing. I invite those energies by calling them out loud (although you can do this silently, too, if you are in a public or shared space), over and over, until they become a little like a chant; this is as close as I get to a rhythm. In between several repeats, I thank the energy for coming and being part of our home as I shake the rattle, dispersing the energy I've called up.

Wrapping Up the Process

It's as simple as that. As with most things, the first time through may feel awkward, but after a few times it will feel very natural and not take long at all. Just like regular cleanings at the dentist help prevent cavities, doing this basic routine on a regular basis will keep your space feeling fresh and supportive. In addition, you'll find that there are fewer and fewer crisis situations that generally send us running for the sage bundle. I suggest putting it on your calendar because time does fly and it's easy to forget. I know from experience.

For eight years, until September 2015, we had a big love bug of a Bernese mountain dog named Norman. Out of all of us who lived in the house, Norman was the most sensitive to the energy in our home. He had a very particular way of behaving that let me know it was time to take care of the energy in the house. After he left us, no one reminded me and I didn't think of it—until, of course, things got really heavy and yucky and we just all felt gross. Pondering what could be wrong, we suddenly realized that Norman wasn't here to be our energetic barometer and it had been many months since I cleared the house.

That goes to show you that it is easy for things to build up until they reach problematic proportions and that even someone who should know better can forget. Now it is on my calendar. I picked the first Friday of each month. I like the idea of starting a month with fresh energy. Friday made sense to me. It is Venus's day (the planet), and Venus is associated with Taurus. Taurus is often known for being stubborn (which, come to think of it, Norman was—both a Taurus *and* stubborn). Taurus is also associated with things that we value, and I do energetic work to help support living my values, so it all makes sense to me. As you know, my ways don't have to be your ways. Think about what makes sense for you.

As a quick checklist, here are the steps in a basic house clearing, containment, and cultivation process:

1. Clearing, part 1: shaking and waking (to loosen up the energy)
2. Clearing, part 2: cleansing (to clear out inappropriate and stagnant energy and to revitalize appropriate energy)
3. Containment: to keep your clean space fresh between cleansings
4. Cultivation: to invite in the energy you want

AIR FRESHENER TECHNIQUES

I call these "air freshener techniques" because they remind me of air fresheners, which help keep things smelling nice between cleanings or work to support specific energy. Under this heading are practices that, from other books I've read, some people do instead of regular cleansings as described above. While that does work for some people, it didn't work for me, which is why I came up with my process. Everyone is different, so try various methods and see what works best for you.

Crystals, stones, and runes can be hidden around a space, under furniture or on doorjambs (maybe secure them with tape or adhesive putty). Depending on the items you select, they can clear, contain, or cultivate specific energy. Don't make the mistake of just buying what someone suggests. Figure out which items feel right for you and make conscious decisions about the purpose they will serve. There are tons of books that list traditional or magical associations, as well as online resources. Some people gather them up once a year and cleanse them by placing them in running water, passing them through sage smoke, or leaving them on a windowsill under a full moon or in sunlight.

Bowls of salt are often hidden around spaces to absorb inappropriate, stagnant, or extremely agitated energy. You can definitely use regular table salt, but many people like pink or Hawaiian red salt. These salts are pink because of a high iron content. Red salt is used in Hawaii to cleanse and bless items and spaces, similar to the way some cultures, particularly Native American, use sage. You can also dissolve salt in water and sprinkle it around the space. One thing I do when I'm hosting either a large number of people or people I don't know well (and consequently am unfamiliar with their energy) is sprinkle salt and put a drop of lavender oil under my welcome mat as a way to cleanse any energy entering my home and to encourage peaceful energy within each individual. You could also do something similar to the threshold of your office, cubicle, or workspace.

Incense or candles, of course, can be lit any time. If you enjoy using these items on a regular basis, it is a simple thing to use them with intention, asking them to cleanse or cultivate as needed. As usual, select incense that supports the energy you are trying to cultivate. Some people like to use candles of particular colors to represent various kinds of energy. There are plenty of color theory resources available. Again, it is most important to pick ones that work for you. For example, red is used for abundance in Chinese color theory. In the US, though, red is usually associated with passion, will, or love, while green (the color of our money and the abundance of the earth) is more often used for prosperity.

Wind chimes on porches or near windows provide bursts of energy as they emit sound. Generally speaking, smaller chimes with lighter tones will create brighter, higher-vibration energy like joy and hope. Deeper chimes will encourage stable, deeply rooted, earthy energy. You can change them out depending on what your needs are or have a few different kinds to create a balanced energetic experience.

I'm all about using materials already at hand, but if you are in a position to invest a little money, tabletop water fountains are so excellent for maintaining flowing, peaceful, light energy, especially the ones that have tiny cymbals in them that randomly make a pleasant sound. Flowing water is, as you may know, an excellent means of cleansing energy, so having constantly moving water in your space will definitely keep things fresh. The light tinkling sounds add a touch of effervescence to the overall energy of the space.

In my experience, the most mundane and best way to encourage clear, flowing, and harmonious energy in a space is to keep the space tidy and physically clean. We know this on a deeply intuitive level. In college my friends and I always laughed about the fact that whenever we were going to sit down to work on an important paper or study for an exam, we always cleaned our rooms. We assumed it was a way to procrastinate, but some part of us knew that our energy and focus would be most supported if we worked in a clean space. Whatever you do, don't have anything in your space that does not support the overall energy that you want to cultivate. The odd knick knack that you dislike but have displayed out of obligation will continue to accrue resentful energy every time you look at it, and consequently it will generate and disperse that energy. In this sense, everything in your home is like an energetic air freshener... and not all the "scents" are pleasant ones.

Adding on to the mundane cleaning theme, what you clean with can affect the energy of your space. Many of us already think about the toxicity issues connected with various cleaning products, and those should definitely be taken into account when selecting cleaning solutions. These are complicated concerns that require a lot of research and individual needs will vary, so I cannot advise on this topic except to say simply be aware of this issue and make conscious choices.

That said, if you use, as many now are, mostly water, vinegar, and baking soda for cleaning, you can add essential oils to invite specific energy. Essential oils are not to be confused with baking extracts. I include that because there was a time when I didn't know that there was a difference. Even if you use more mainstream cleaning products, you can simply do another pass over the cleaned surfaces with water and essential oils. I wouldn't add essential oils to mainstream chemical cleaners because I don't know if there would any adverse reactions. Before you use peppermint (or any oil) on a surface, do a spot test first to make sure no damage occurs. Use caution with adding oils because a little goes a long way. Early on in my energy-focused housekeeping, I heard that peppermint oil attracts abundance. That made sense to me because mint spreads like crazy; it is the epitome of abundance! So I washed my floors with water and peppermint essential oil.

I went a little overboard on the peppermint because my house smelled like a tube of toothpaste had exploded in there. Good thing it was spring and I could open the windows.

Floors are not the only thing you can clean using water and essential oils. Other key areas are window sills, doorjambs and casings, and baseboards. These areas are often neglected in general, and as small, ignored horizontal surfaces, energy can get stuck there. Also, because doors are where lots of energy comes in and goes out of a space, having a threshold that cleanses and enhances is helpful. I think of it as a metaphysical carwash that prepares whoever goes in or comes out to be their very best.

You will see essential oil blends on the market such as thieves oil, which is a specific blend and is used for cleansing and purification. Florida water, which includes essential oils, is actually alcohol-based (so take care around flames) and is used for many purposes, from purification to protection to easing depression. I have not used either thieves oil or Florida water, preferring to use single-note essential oils or custom blends that I create for my specific purposes. However, these are both popularly used and deserve a mention in any book on energy work.

There is a product that goes by various names—blueing, anil, and Reckitt's Crown Blue Squares—that is used in laundry to make things white. Some folk magic traditions use this product. Dissolve a square in water. Put the water in dishes throughout the space (as you would with salt) or sprinkle around (as mentioned in the clearing section above) for cleansing and protection. I've not tried these myself but know people who swear by them.

Himalayan salt lamps are very popular and are said to do everything from cleansing energy to energizing a space to promoting sleep to enhancing focus. I don't know if they can do all that, but I do know that salt and light are both excellent means of clearing energy. There are other ways of having salt in a space, but like the tabletop water fountain, this could be a nice investment piece if you find that salt works well for you. Try bowls of salt first before investing in a salt lamp.

Another product I've not tried are camphor blocks, which some people use by placing the block in a bowl of water and placing the bowl under the bed to cleanse the energy of the house. These old folk remedies are so interesting, but for me, if there is no resonance, then it doesn't make sense to use it. Also, I like telling people not to buy things when everyday home items will do. But still, don't be afraid to be open to new ideas. You never know until you try, and if your curiosity is pulling you toward something, there may be a reason. Trust your instincts.

I mention these last few products so if you research online or go to a local metaphysical store, you won't be surprised or caught off-guard. When people find a product that works for them, they love to share their enthusiasm. That's great, and we can often find new things that work well for us, too. However, enthusiasm can cross the line to evangelism, causing people to claim that this or that product is hands-down the best at whatever it is you want to do. I want you to know that isn't necessarily true. Something like Florida water, for example, has deep cultural ties with the South and Hoodoo. People who resonate with that sensibility, whether or not they were raised in it or practice it, would probably enjoy greater success with Florida water. For a Midwest girl such as myself, however, there isn't as much resonance, so it likely wouldn't be better than anything else I could use. If there was one thing that worked equally well for everyone, we'd know it because, honestly, who wouldn't prefer an easy, 100 percent reliable answer to trial and error, experimentation, and hard work? So be open and curious, but also be sensible.

Sample Energy Work Schedule
for Spaces

DAILY
- make bed
- evening tidy-up

WEEKLY
- regular house cleaning with intention

MONTHLY
- house clearing (as described in this chapter)

YEARLY
- protection work: salt around parameter, acorns in windowsills, mojo bags for cars, recharge runes for purses, bags, and suitcases

AS NEEDED
- clearing after clients, preparing welcome mats, incense, candles

PORTABLE ENERGY TOOLS

People often wear or carry symbolic items for specific purposes, such as a lucky coin or affirmation tucked in a wallet, a small crystal in a pocket, or an amulet worn as jewelry. We don't always think of these as part of energy work, but they are. The lucky coin is meant to attract energy that is favorable to our endeavors. An affirmation can remind us to focus on honoring our own power. An amulet draws to us the type of energy it was designed to attract, such as protection. Some people put several items into a tiny pouch called a mojo bag. Anything can be charged with the intent to attract or repel energy.

Each year when I do my annual property line and window protection, I always refresh my portable items. For our vehicles, I use a snack-sized baggie containing salt, an acorn, and a rune with the Eolh symbol on it. I made the runes with one of those clay products that are baked in the oven, such as Sculpey clay. All three items are for protection. When I made the runes, I made plenty extra to have on hand. I carry one in my purse and always put one in each piece of luggage I carry while traveling.

Protection is not the only purpose for these portable energy attractors. A small rose quartz can impart loving energy. A little bit of lavender can encourage a sense of calm. A tarot or oracle card, or even a piece of paper with a word written on it, can cultivate the energy it represents. Portable energy tools are not limited to items you carry. I know women who polish their nails with specific colors or wear certain scents that represent the kind of energy they want to express in the world. As cheesy as it may sound, a smile or a kind word can be powerful energy generators.

I do enjoy and use portable energy items in my daily life, but they are like an accessory because the most effective energy work that you can do as you move through your day and through the world is managing your own energy body. Do not feel like you have to create and carry something with you all the time. You already do; you are a walking portable energy generator, dispenser, and director. Speaking of being a walking energetic creator, it is now time to move on to one of the most exciting and important aspects of working with energy: manifesting change in the world by being a walking blessing.

CHAPTER 10

CO-CREATING THE WORLD
THROUGH BLESSINGS

Do you feel powerful? If you've done even a few of the suggestions shared thus far, you should. You're changing yourself from someone bound by the past, prone to reacting rather than responding, and separated from your values to someone who is free, who responds consciously to the world and others, and who is the living embodiment of their soul's purpose. You're changing your environment from one of stagnant and inappropriate energy to a space of freely flowing, healthy energy that supports your core values.

The work you are doing is magical and amazing. If that is all you did, that would be enough to make anyone feel proud. But there is something more you can do: participate in creating a harmonious future. I think this is something that can only be done effectively by people who have set themselves free and learned to master their own energy. Indeed, I sometimes suspect that all the evil in the world is perpetuated by those who have not done their shadow work. I think this is true partly because until we are free and responsive rather than controlled and reactive, we can't see very far past our own issues—not because we are selfish clods but because we are wounded, fragile, and requiring help, not judgment. Also, it takes a certain level of confidence bred by experience to step into this opportunity.

Helping create the future is really the logical progression from creating (or, more accurately, revealing) yourself and managing your personal environment. It is also a gift and an honor. Furthermore, it is the responsibility of everyone who walks this planet. Whether we are conscious of it or not, we are all, through our actions and inactions, creating the future. If you are alive, you are creating, whether you know it or not. Most people move through the world manifesting and creating without realizing it.

You, though, are aware of your power. It is said that with great power comes great responsibility. By neglecting this aspect of energy work, you are denying your potential and denying the world of the energetic medicine that you can provide. You don't have to wait until you are completely healed or trained to do this work; you can and should start now. You are here to express your humanity as a walking blessing to all life. Trust me, after all the hard work you've done already, this will feel like play. In fact, it makes me feel like a modern-day Santa, bestowing gifts on the world just for the joy of it. I hope you find that same fulfillment as you sprinkle your own magic throughout the world.

CREATING THE WORLD

I promised that this part would be fun, and it is. But first I do have to share some important ideas that aren't necessarily the fun part. After this section we are done with the hard stuff. Don't skip this, though, because you want your work to be as effective as possible.

Generous orthodoxy is a contemporary, radical Christian movement that can be applied in your life no matter your spiritual path or lack thereof. Those who practice generous orthodoxy are transforming traditional Christian dogma to be more open, flexible, and loving. There is, of course, much more to it, but here we are only concerned with the general principle. That principle is that in order to heal something, you must love it. This can be the most challenging part of creating the future through healthy energy work. It requires us to move past the duality of us versus them— past the things that divide us, past emotional reactiveness, past mental judgment. It asks us to remember that everyone is walking around wounded, scared, and anxious, and that judgment and attack only create further damage. Generous orthodoxy depends on healthy discernment and loving motives. For those of us interested in helping heal the world (and everyone in it) and in creating a better, healthier future for all life, we have to love this world and its inhabitants as they are, just as we can only heal ourselves by starting from a place of love.

When we think about changing the world, we often focus on our healthy actions as the ones that affect the world without realizing that *all* our actions, whether loving, unhealthy, or malicious, create change. I believe this is true, and it is an important reason to take care of our own wounds and issues. If we are toggling between trying really hard to do a few good deeds and raging at the world around us, it is like our actions cancel each other out.

Remember the story of the boy asking his grandfather about the two wolves? It's like that. I'm told it's also like field theory. Energy is always flowing through us. While it is in us, we shape it, give it character and flavor, and transform it before we release it back into the world with our every action, deeply held beliefs, and nourished emotions. I differentiate between deeply held thoughts (or, as I described earlier, "entertained" thoughts) and fleeting thoughts. Fleeting thoughts are ideas and suggestions that present themselves and that we can choose to entertain or let float by. Entertained or deeply held thoughts are ones we cultivate or feed. Likewise, nourished emotions are different from experienced emotions in that just because we have an emotion doesn't mean we are nourishing and holding it; we have learned through our energy work that we can release the emotion back to the earth for transformation and redistribution.

I think this is important to understand because sometimes it feels like ideas such as the law of attraction can be taken to extremes and cause us to live in fear of our thoughts and feelings. I know that I've been on the receiving end of good-intentioned people calling me out for using what they consider a negative word. To me, the universe is not a lawyer looking for some loophole or misstep to punish us. I don't want you to live in anxiety worrying about making some horrendous mistake that will create disharmony in the world by using a certain word or having a fleeting emotion. That kind of thinking is distracting at best and paralyzing at worst.

Our momentary thoughts and feelings are not necessarily feeding the disharmonious wolf. However, if thoughts or feelings have been cultivated in us enough to manifest as actions, words, belief systems, and emotional expressions, they do feed one wolf or the other. This affects our own energy body as well as the energetic tendencies in the world.

Let's just take a moment to remember that even when we aren't practicing good energy cultivation, we are still cultivating energy. It happens in little ways that have a cumulative effect. Cursing or yelling at other drivers on the road may seem like a benign way to vent since usually no one else hears us, and perhaps there are some psychological studies that prove this. But I think that the long-term costs, to ourselves and the world, outweigh the benefits. Plus, there are other ways to manage frustrated energy, as you know. Expressing such rage and frustration feeds that energy within and influences the energy around us. I can't judge if that energy is appropriate or inappropriate for anyone else. We all decide what energy supports our values and beliefs, but I'm willing to bet that rage and frustration are not high on anyone's list of important life values.

Paying attention to this can be challenging, particularly when we are face to face with people or ideas that are contrary to our beliefs. For example, if we believe in marriage equality, when we talk with someone who does not, it is so easy to think about them with judgment rather than with curiosity. But whenever we say something like, "How can they even think that? How can they be so stupid?" we are contributing to the energetic tendency of bullying. Our intent may be to support acceptance but because our words and beliefs are fueled by judgment, we are doing nothing to further the cause of tolerance—quite the opposite.

This ties in to the concept of generous orthodoxy because we must remember to act from a place of energetic harmony, which does not include judgment but does feature curiosity. Instead of asking "How can they even think that? How can they be so stupid?" we might ask, with sincerity, "Can you please tell me more about your beliefs?" In doing so, we could discover the root of this belief, perhaps due to severe emotional wounding through a damaging religious upbringing. We can see past the angry adult to the scared child afraid of being separated from his family by being sent to hell. We are more apt to create a future that features harmonious acceptance if we attend to the wounded child rather than argue with the angry adult.

We probably cannot dialogue directly with that inner child, but we can create an energetic tendency that will eventually foster healing. It takes time—sometimes a long time. For example, if you have a relative or coworker or acquaintance who has opinions opposed to your own, instead of rolling your eyes or making an eloquent, impassioned speech, just listen. Then ask curious

and respectful questions and listen some more. Don't try to promote your agenda; give them space to unfold their ideas. Let them
come to know you as a safe person to talk to. As you extend them
respect and curiosity, they will probably eventually extend the
same to you. A bridge is created where you can discuss rather
than argue. You find areas of agreement and build from there. You
may discover that you share common goals but still differ on how
to achieve them. This may sound like a small thing, but in a world
where people from different political parties cannot even talk to
each other, it is an important step.

In this world of instant gratification, I know it can be hard to
be patient and do the deep work of creating the future. Trust me,
I fall short of my own values every day. The important thing is
to keep moving in the right direction, and when we get offtrack,
we, like a good airplane pilot, correct our course. Energy work
is a long game. In fact, there seems to be an opportunity for an
even deeper and broader level of this work that I've only recently
learned about. It's something I've experienced, not read about,
and I am still in the process of figuring it out. If you are curious,
please see appendix B.

To end on a happier note, just as our actions can cause unin-
tended energetic shifts that are contrary to our ideals, small
actions that support your values can feed into exciting and harmonious energetic fields. A friend of mine, Sasha, gave a wonderful
presentation about tarot and magic and the power of courageously
facing your shadow at a conference I attended. She gave everyone who attended a tiny shaker of glitter with a word or phrase
attached. Those little gifts were her way of extending her energy
into the world. One attendee, another friend of mine, received one
that said "movement."

This friend was in the midst of a life crisis, knowing she needed to change or do something but unsure of exactly what she wanted. Within two months she decided to quit her job, pack up her car, and embark on a quest to find her true self. Within six months she put her plan in motion. Her last act before she drove away was to sprinkle her car and herself with the glitter from that tiny shaker. That small thing—a bit of glitter and a tag that said "movement"—became part of the energy field that led my friend to move, to shake up the energy of her life.

I'm sure Sasha had no idea exactly how her energetic action would play out; she simply lived her values, gave from the best that was within her, and deeply affected in a harmonious and beautiful way the life of at least one other person. You never know what small action will become part of a larger shift. Even if you feel like you can't take big actions, you can still be part of shifting the tendency of the world toward harmony.

BLESSINGS

For the last few years, giving blessings has been my favorite thing to do. It began one fall when I was in intense shamanic training for a winter solstice ritual. The other students and I were trained as blessers. We learned how to ask our allies, helping spirits, and the world around us to lend us their energy for the purpose of blessing the ritual attendees. Of course, part of the training included preparing ourselves by attending to our own energy bodies. The work was so amazing and gratifying that I continued to study the art of blessing on my own after the course was completed. My main text was John O'Donohue's *To Bless the Space Between Us*, a wonderful book full of grace and wisdom.

You may wonder "What does blessing people have to do with energy work?" I started thinking that blessing was a kind of energy work when I was trained to ask spirits and nature to lend me their energy. As I continued on with my explorations, I wondered how blessings differed from prayers. They share some similarities, and in some ways prayer is also energy work. Blessing others is characterized by more proactive and empowering aspects than prayer, an important difference that appeals to me. A blessing is given to someone (or many someones) directly, which seems more personal and intimate, while a prayer is a dialogue with the Divine on behalf of someone. A blessing is something that you bestow, a movement of energy toward someone, while a prayer requests action on someone's behalf. A blessing is a direct way of co-creating, while prayer is one step removed from immediate involvement. Also, I like the poetic, gentle, gracious feel of blessings.

In this book I strove to use the most neutral language possible. I'm taking a risk by using the word "blessing," because it is so dear to my heart. If the word doesn't feel right to you, I hope you mentally replace "blessing" with "energy work" or whatever phrase best suits you.

HOW TO BLESS

Before we discuss how to bless, we should establish the rules about who can bless. Do you have to be trained or ordained? Do you have to achieve a certain level of energetic harmony? Do you have to be practically perfect? Luckily, the answer is no. The truth is that anyone can bless. If someone sneezes and someone else replies "God bless you," a blessing has been given. If a friend is leaving on a trip and you say "Safe travels," you have bestowed a blessing. Some blessings are given without much intention or conscious thought, such as the often perfunctory response to a sneeze.

Blessings happen all the time and are always sweet, welcome dewdrops of harmonious energy. So why, for example, did a group of us train to bless at a solstice ritual? I suppose it is for the same reason someone trains for anything: to get better at it. Almost anyone can follow directions and bake a cake, draw a picture of a house, or sing. People who want to get better, faster, more efficient, or achieve a specific result in any area, such as baking, drawing, or singing, train. The training may include classes or instruction through books or YouTube videos. Training always requires practice. It doesn't matter how much you read; if you don't practice, you won't improve. The same is true of blessing. Admittedly, there aren't many training programs for blessing, nor many books that teach the art form. For becoming more adept at blessing, your training includes the skills in energy clearing, containment, and cultivation that you've already developed and practice. The next few paragraphs will help, too.

To be honest, I think one of the many reasons I love blessing is that it is so easy but has such an awesome payoff in terms of personal satisfaction. Have you ever made a simple recipe that people rave over and think was super hard? Or crafted an item that was super easy but looked really artistic? Or, even better, have you ever had a day when you kind of just rolled out of bed and put on some comfortable, handy clothes, only to have everyone you meet compliment you? For me, blessing feels like those kinds of experiences—almost like it is unfair to get such compliments (in the case of the recipe) or to feel so big and warm in the heart (in the case of blessing) for such little effort.

Let's break down the steps of a blessing as I do them, not because blessing has a codified process but rather to make it easier to develop your process. Also, these steps are not rigid; my blessings often arise from my heart spontaneously and just happen.

This technique reflects the most common order in which I usually do things. A blessing needs four things: energy, a recipient, intent, and a medium.

Energy

To bestow an effective blessing, you need to cultivate the kind of energy that would appropriately animate the blessing. Because the blessings you give will be in line with your values, you are already cultivating this energy, so no extra work is needed there. You don't have to worry about depleting your energy because energy is meant to flow. As it flows out of you, more flows in. The energy that comes in is cleared and cultivated through your personal energy practice and is ready to be released again into the world. Another good reason to keep your energy harmonious is that you will always have what you need whenever unplanned blessings need to happen.

In addition to the energy within your energy body, you can draw on other energy, as I was trained to do for the solstice ritual. Be careful about what you draw from, as you don't want to bring in energy that isn't appropriate for your task. I've never drawn energy from another person and wouldn't recommend it. Some people call that psychic vampirism, whether permission is granted or not, and it probably isn't something that falls within the category of your values and ideals. Besides that, you cannot know for sure the state of another person's energy unless you are a trained energy worker. I mostly draw from nature, particularly trees in my area with whom I've developed a relationship.

While I have drawn energy from ancestors and spirit allies in my shamanic training, I don't do that now in my personal practice. There are theoretical reasons that don't pertain here, but another reason is that it doesn't feel necessary. There is plenty of energy in this world, and adding another layer or step complicates something that can be simple, elegant, and easy. If you are going to ask nature to lend you energy, always ask permission and remember to say thank you when you are done. However, since this is a book for beginners, the simplest thing—and it is what I generally do—is to rely on your energy. Honestly, you are enough.

Recipient

In addition to the energy, you need a recipient for the blessing. You can bless a single person, a few people, or a huge group of people. You can even bless the whole world and every single person in it. People aren't the only things that can benefit from being blessed. Animals, particularly pets who seem to bless us so much just by being in our lives, are lovely to bless. Items, places, projects, communications, and events can also be blessed, such as cars, homes, a book, a letter, or weddings. Sometimes I bless an email or letter, sending it with love and understanding. I've blessed manuscripts, asking that they have value for those who read the completed books. Because everything that exists is made of energy, everything is affected by and can benefit from the infusion of appropriate, harmonious energy. Whatever you think can benefit from a blessing probably can.

It is important to keep in mind the idea of generous orthodoxy. Our relationship with or attitude toward the recipient is vital. O'Donohue (the author of *To Bless the Space Between Us*, mentioned above) says, "Wherever one person takes another into the care of their heart, they have the power to bless."[7] Unless you take the recipient into the sphere of your love, your power to bless will be inhibited.

---

7   John O'Donohue, *To Bless the Space Between Us* (New York: Doubleday, 2008), 207.

We have to pause and consider the question of permission: Do we need permission to bestow blessings on people? In magical work it is considered unethical to do magic on behalf of people without their permission. With other sorts of more formalized energy work, such as Reiki, practitioners do not work on people without getting consent. Does blessing someone require prior approval? This is a question you will have to answer for yourself. Because I am also a magic worker and because I think that energy work and magic are extremely closely entwined, you'd think I'd struggle with this issue more. Oddly enough, I do not. I will never do magic for someone without their agreement, yet I feel completely fine about blessing anyone and everyone and not even mentioning it. We walk through our days affecting the energy of everyone around us, just as everyone else's energy affects us. No one is asking permission; that would be quite impossible, as most of the energy being expressed is not being done so in a conscious manner anyhow. Sometimes things are complicated, but we make the best decisions we can. For now, I will bless the world without qualms or hesitation.

Intent

The purpose of a blessing is, ideally, to bestow beneficial, appropriate energy. Blessings can be a wish for general goodwill or, in words that Pagan practitioners will recognize, "the greatest good of all beings." There can never be too much goodwill in the world, so if you ever just feel a rising up of affection for the world but aren't sure how to bestow it, release the energy as a blessing for goodwill.

Blessings can also, of course, be specific. People can use blessings for safe travel, finding strength in a hard time, or direction when feeling lost. Cars can be blessed for safety and smooth operation. Homes can be blessed for anything you wish to cultivate in that space. There is the question of how we know whether a specific energy is appropriate or harmonious for the recipient. Just because something is right for us doesn't mean it's right for someone else. I rely on discernment, common sense, and faith. I do my best to figure out if I think a blessing is appropriate and bestow it with the intention that it is for the recipient's greatest good. We are asking hard questions about metaphysical energy, which we cannot know about with certainty, and about human beings, who are really complicated. I say we all do our best and believe that we are moving toward healing and harmony.

Medium

The intention, once formed, needs a medium in order to bestow it—or, in other words, to manifest it in the world. Most blessings are shaped by words, which can be written or spoken; if silence is appropriate, thought works too. Blessings can also be given through song, music, or touch. If you want to bless through touch, always make sure to ask permission first. Unlike whether or not you can bless without permission, it is never okay to touch someone without permission. In this book, we will focus on words in order to keep it simple. Once you've used words, and if you feel led, you can explore using music or touch or even anointing with oil or water. There is plenty of space for creativity in blessing.

Blessings can be poetic or they can be simple and straightforward. I think a blessing should reflect the best part of yourself, even if that part isn't fully manifested. By giving it expression through blessing, you help it come more fully into being. The exact words or cadence or lack thereof are not important; however, the word "may" is commonly used in blessings. John O'Donohue explains why. He does use Christian language, but don't let that put you off. He means exactly what we've been discussing in these pages. I'll unpack the language after the quote.

> The language of blessing is invocation, a calling forth. This is why the word *may* occurs ...; it is a word of benediction. It imagines and wills the fulfillment of desire. In the evocation of our blessings here, the word *may* is the spring through which the Holy Spirit is invoked to surge into presence and effect. The Holy Spirit is the subtle presence and secret energy behind every blessing here.[8]

O'Donohue uses the word *may* because it is a word of benediction, which also means to bestow. When he says "it imagines and wills the fulfillment of desire," he means the same thing we do when we gather and direct energy. The idea that *may* is the opening through which the Holy Spirit is invoked and surges into presence is a different way of saying that *may* is the means by which we guide energy in a way that affects the world. While he says that the Holy Spirit is the energy behind his blessings, we say that metaphysical energy, cultivated by us, animates our blessings.

This is an example of what I mean when I say so many spiritual principles are shared by different paths. Sometimes language causes us to miss that. It is a shame to let beautiful truths pass us by because of semantics, but it's understandable, especially when someone has been wounded by a specific tradition. If that's the case, we pass it by until we find it expressed in words that don't turn us off. So despite the completeness and loveliness of O'Donohue's description of the function of *may* in blessings, I will add mine. Rather than thinking of *may* as an opening, I think of it as a magic wand that allows me to shape and guide the energy exactly as I wish.

8   Ibid., xvi.

Don't feel obligated to use the word *may*. Your blessings should reflect your unique gifts. It isn't even necessary to have a specific word or formula. Some people like to have a method because it is easier to create something with a foundation or template. Others prefer complete artistic freedom. If you are interested in reading extraordinary blessings, do check out O'Donohue's book. If you are interested in seeing ordinary blessings, I've included some that I've bestowed in appendix A. In the meantime, let's explore some creative ways to share our harmonious energy in the world.

CREATIVE BLESSING PRACTICES

Bestowing the gift of energy can be done simply just by speaking it to a person or writing it in a card. Sometimes blessings are given to a group at an event or celebration. Those are wonderful ways to share your carefully cultivated energy with others and with the world. As we go about our days, we can't help but notice how badly we are in need of blessings. We only have to see a stressed-out coworker, a confused friend, the angry energy of people in a long line, or any number of news headlines flowing through our media every single day to find places ripe for blessing. Once you start experiencing the glorious satisfaction of energy work and as you begin to come into closer alignment with your values and ideals, you'll want to do more. Here are some ways you can do that. Maybe they'll inspire more ideas that you can try.

One of my very favorite things to do is to bless my neighborhood before I go to sleep. It started out rather selfishly. My wife was away on a very extended journey and I got in the habit of directing energy toward the edges of our property for protection. One evening I wondered if I could push my energy farther. Trying it out and finding that I could, I thought I might as well protect as many of the homes around me as I could. Little by little, day by day, the practice changed from just protection. Instead, I bestowed other energy, other blessings, each night a different one. I thought of them as seeds that were being planted and in time would grow, eventually spreading even farther.

As the weather grew colder (it gets very cold in Minnesota) and thoughts of those without homes wrung my heart, I added a blessing for comfort and warmth. Throughout the winter, every night, I blessed the neighborhood with warmth plus another blessing. I continue this work still; it has become an important part of my routine, one I look forward to. Every night the blessing is different, and I never know ahead of time what the blessing will be. Inspiration always comes like some wise and caring being whispering in my ear. Even though no one hears the blessing, it feels like some of the most powerful work I've ever done.

One night something interesting happened. After I finished the blessing but was still looking out of the window, I saw a car driving out of the neighborhood. As it was driving away, I immediately thought toward the people in the car: "And you—you are taking this blessing with you and spreading it wherever you go; it is going viral." It feels good knowing that no matter how small, I am doing something to help make the world a better place. That is one of the many gifts of blessing.

In addition to making me feel really good about myself, sometimes blessing makes me feel like an undercover agent for healing and harmony. Long ago I learned a method of spellwork whereby you charge a small action, such as crossing your fingers, as a way to silently and quickly cast a spell. That technique applies very well to energy work and blessing. Just as the word *may* is considered a spring, portal, or wand, I created a movement—simply making an "okay" sign with my index finger and thumb and then flicking my index finger—that would be, in essence, a wand dispersing the energy of a blessing. When I'm out and about and I pass people, nobody notices the motion as I silently bless them. I also sometimes use a smile in the same way, although that is more noticeable as I try to make eye contact in those cases. The finger flicks are just little blessings, like a happy surprise or a treat. The smiles are slightly more intimate. Either way, I'm out there spreading as much goodwill as possible through living my values and blessing everyone I can. If you, dear reader, start doing this too, can you imagine the future we are helping to create?

A friend of mine blesses all the money that passes through her hands so that when it goes from person to person, she is spreading generosity and prosperity. You can do this with anything. Blessing food that you are sharing with others is a great way to do this. If you make the food yourself, you can imbue it with energy to nourish souls as well as bodies. Cookies or other treats made for potlucks, office parties, or cookie exchanges, for example, can be charged with sweetness. Who couldn't use a little more sweetness in their life? Food, money, gifts...you can put your energy into anything, making the item even more special.

CONCLUSION

There are so many opportunities to spread healthy, appropriate, and harmonious energy throughout our world. You are a beautiful being with such power and ability. Through a kind word, a generous act, or moment of understanding, by cultivating emotional acceptance, by developing curiosity, you can clear, contain, and cultivate energy. By doing so, you will more fully and easily live your values in every word and action, thereby living your soul's purpose and creating a world supportive of all life. If the future is bright, it is because your unique magic is part of its creation.

I began working on this book toward the end of the 2016 election cycle. Events of the day definitely affected how I thought about energy, including the most important application of our energy work: healing the world. It occurred to me that the great rift that divides us grows stronger because we are feeding it. We have been feeding the wolf of division. Now we can start feeding the wolf of health, peace, and love. You've read this far. You understand that this is the real reason we do this work: to get to this point where we can, with a flick of a finger or a heart-driven blessing, be part of the solution. Until we calm down, focus, and start consciously making decisions about what we are creating, our beautiful world is going to continue to move further and further away from peace and wholeness. With your skills and most of all with your commitment to seeing the world, really seeing it, you are now part of the conscious change, part of the restoration of harmony on this planet. You are a walking blessing. You carry magic. Just like the farmer and his bag of magic sand, you will change your world.

May you know your power and worth.
May you take the world into the care of your heart.
May you know the joy of living your soul's desire.
May you go in grace and peace.

APPENDIX A

A SAMPLING OF BLESSINGS

May your guiding star be bright and clear.
May it direct your steps.
May it infuse your words.
May it fill your heart.

May you find and face the darkest parts of yourself.
May you find the peace and strength to transform them.
May you discover your next best step on your journey to live your true soul's purpose.
May you know that you have the power to change yourself and the world.

May the magic in your world leap into your heart like drops of fire and pulse through your veins, making you feel just so good to be alive.

May you move through this season with ease and grace as a walking blessing to the whole world.

May you find sparkly joy in small moments.
May your steps lead to wonders that delight your heart.

May you find the heart center of your life.
May your mind be filled with beautiful ideas, and may the
*   sweetness of your heart lovingly nurture them.*

May you find happiness in being human even when it isn't
*   pleasant.*

May words of wisdom drift to you on the wind.
May you breathe them in deeply.
May they encourage and guide you.
And may your words encourage and guide your fellow
*   travelers as we all walk each other home.*

May autumn wrap the last warmth of summer's memories
*   around you like a hug.*
May autumn's bright sweetness inspire your muse to dance
*   around like champagne bubbles.*
May these gloriously beautiful days lead you gently and
*   kindly toward winter like a trusted friend.*

May you be visited by Brigid the healer.
May some small wound be healed and an essential part of
*   your soul recovered.*

a sampling of blessings

May the earth's deep dark cradle your soul.

May the stars' gentle light comfort your spirit.

May the Divine's love flow through your life.

May you have the courage to know your power.

May you have the wisdom to know how to use it.

May you have the heart to know why to use it.

APPENDIX B

SERVING THE OLD BONE MOTHER

They say if you want to really learn something, teach it. In my experience this is true. If I've been doing or practicing something for a while, nothing encourages me more to sort out my thoughts and get super clear on a topic than planning a workshop or writing a book. Even though I often think I have a strong foundation and full picture, slowing down and making sure that everything is explained so that the people who are not in my head can understand the ideas shows me the gaps in my own thinking, forcing me to probe further, to flesh out all the concepts. Another experience teachers and authors have while planning and writing is that their own knowledge and experience grows in unplanned ways.

This information is in an appendix because it doesn't quite fit into the basic beginner-level scope of this book and yet it was so fascinating that I really wanted to share it with you. This is not instruction; this is simply information. I cannot provide instruction as I am only dipping my toe in this vast, dark ocean as I finish writing the manuscript. There has not been enough time and experience to claim enough mastery to instruct others.

In December and January 2016/2017 there were some days when I was unaccountably sad. Not just sad but heartbroken, weeping, with anger and frustration mingled in. There was nothing wrong with me or in my life, and it didn't feel like my sadness. It felt like I was carrying or holding sadness. After fighting it for several days, I gave myself over to it, expressing the feelings with tears and stomping feet, pitiful vocalizing, and angry sounds. It didn't really take long before it was all gone and I felt like a heavy, wet blanket was removed from me. I should note that I was walking my dog around the lake near our house in the early morning winter darkness.

A few steps after the wet blanket feeling left, I had one of those delicious revelations that are such a joyful relief the moment they arrive. Of course, once it entered my consciousness, I thought it was pretty obvious. But isn't that the way of revelations?

I mentioned the winter solstice ritual training I'd done where I learned how to bless. There was another aspect of that training and that ritual that I didn't mention, one that is even more powerful to me than blessing, and by now you know how I feel about blessing. In the mythology created by my teacher there is the Old Bone Mother, a being who moves over the world as the solstice approaches; you can hear her in the rustling autumn leaves. She gathers up all the old stuff that people don't need anymore—all the stale emotions, limiting ideas, and destructive practices—and takes them home with her. She sits up all solstice night knitting new things out of the trash she collected—new things to give back to the world as the light returns.

The first half of the solstice ritual was devoted to the Old Bone Mother, telling her story and then reenacting it. In ritual, people were given the opportunity to interact with the Old Bone Mother and let her take what they no longer needed. This took a while since there were over one hundred people at each ritual (we ran the ritual for three nights). While this was going on, the other trainees and I sat on the stage, covered in black cloths, creating this mournful, keening, deep wall of sound the whole time. It was such a strange and powerful experience. It really felt like we were serving a goddess or some powerful spirit. The saddest thing was how I assumed that unless I participated in the training each year (the only way to be part of the ritual), which would not be feasible as it is a huge time commitment, I might never do that work again.

My mistake was in thinking that it was the form of the work that was important: the ritual setting, the time of year, the chanting with others. Under the form, though, is the actual work, and that, like blessing work or clearing, can take so many forms. I realized that through the expansion of my blessing work and my sincere desire to serve the world, I was being shown a deeper, darker way to serve. I was being shown how to attend to the work of the Old Bone Mother at any time, in different ways. The sadness that overcame me was not my personal sadness. It was a collective sadness, a shared energy that was inappropriate at that time, either because hope was needed rather than sadness or that there was just too much sadness... since I wasn't sure what was going on until after the fact, I'm not perfectly sure which was the case.

This work reminded me of other practices I've heard of, such as intercessory prayer or sin eating. Neither are exactly the same, but the general idea is that someone takes on an experience in the place of another. When there is a surfeit of collective energy, there are, I am sure, people in the world who take it into themselves, feel it, experience it, and give themselves over to it so that they can gather it and channel it back into the earth to be redistributed as needed. It makes sense that someone devoting themselves to a blessing practice would move into this sort of work. This is clearing work; as you know, you have to clear, to make space, before you can cultivate different energy.

As I mentioned, I'm just at the beginning of this journey so I can't share much more about it, as it is still a mystery to me. If you find yourself being pulled in this direction, I'd love to hear from you and maybe we can learn from each other.

Although I can't share much in the way of instruction, I will say this: if you pursue this work, do make sure you protect yourself energetically. You may be pulling some very "not everyday"–type energy through you. Clear, contain, and cultivate. Use whatever protection techniques work for you. Decording, visualizing cleansing light followed by fire, and holding a tiger's-eye stone are my go-to techniques when working with energies I'm not familiar with. We haven't really talked about transmuting energy in this book, partly because it is not beginner-level material and partly because beyond giving the energy back to the earth, I don't have a deep understanding or experience of this kind of work. However, I've found that using sound seems to help this process—this taking in, feeling, and releasing work. Maybe it is because it is the type of work I am most uncomfortable with or maybe it is some other reason, but using my own voice in ways that seem strange (keening, moaning, weeping) feels the most appropriate. Most important for me is identifying, feeling/honoring, and releasing because the energy is so overwhelming and clearly not "mine." It is work I am honored to do, but also I don't want to hold that energy longer than necessary. If you cannot find a way to release it, ask your concept of the Divine or your higher self or the universe to take it from you, and follow that request by decording and/or doing the water visualization for clearing your chakras. You can't take care of the world if you don't take care of yourself.

BIBLIOGRAPHY

Books

Bell, Rob. *Love Wins: A Book About Heaven, Hell, and the Fate of Every Person Who Ever Lived*. New York: Harper Collins, 2011.

———. *What We Talk About When We Talk About God*. New York: Harper Collins, 2013.

Brennan, Barbara Ann. *Hands of Light: A Guide to Healing Through the Human Energy Field*. New York: Bantam, 1988.

Campbell, Joseph, with Bill Moyers. *The Power of Myth*. New York: Doubleday, 1988.

Chauran, Alexandra. *Have You Been Hexed? Recognizing and Breaking Curses*. Woodbury, MN: Llewellyn, 2013.

Cunningham, Scott and David Harrington. *The Magical Household: Spells and Rituals for the Home*. Woodbury, MN: Llewellyn, 1983/2008.

Faivre, Antione. *The Eternal Hermes: From Greek God to Alchemical Magus*, trans. Joscelyn Godwin. Grand Rapids, MI: Phanes Press, 1995.

Gilbert, Elizabeth. *Big Magic: Creative Living Beyond Fear*. New York: Penguin, 2016.

Harpur, Patrick. *The Philosopher's Secret Fire: A History of the Imagination*. Chicago, IL: Ivan R. Dee Press, 2002.

Hyde, Lewis. *Trickster Makes the World: Mischief, Myth, and Art*. New York: Farrer, Straus, and Giroux, 2010.

Linn, Denise. *Sacred Space: Clearing and Enhancing the Energy of Your Home*. New York: Random House, 1995.

Meyer, Jaime. *Drumming the Soul Awake*. Minneapolis, MN: Jaime Meyer, 2008.

Mickaharic, Draja. *Spiritual Cleansing: A Handbook of Psychic Protection*. San Francisco, CA: Weiser Books, 1982/2012.

Moore, Thomas. *A Religion of One's Own: A Guide to Creating a Personal Spirituality in a Secular World*. New York: Gotham Books, 2014.

O'Donohue, John. *Eternal Echoes: Celtic Reflections on Our Yearning to Belong*. New York: Perennial, 1999.

———. *To Bless the Space Between Us: A Book of Blessings*. New York: Doubleday, 2008.

Penczak, Christopher. *The Inner Temple of Witchcraft: Magick, Meditation, and Psychic Development*. Woodbury, MN: Llewellyn, 2002.

———. *The Outer Temple of Witchcraft: Circles, Spells, and Rituals*. Woodbury, MN: Llewellyn, 2004.

———. *The Temple of Shamanic Witchcraft: Shadows, Spirits, and the Healing Journey*. Woodbury, MN: Llewellyn, 2005.

Salisbury, David. *A Mystic Guide to Cleansing and Clearing*. Winchester, UK: Moon Books, 2016.

Whitehurst, Tess. *Magical Housekeeping: Simple Charms and Practical Tips for Creating a Harmonious Home*. Woodbury, MN: Llewellyn, 2014.

Podcasts (all available on iTunes)

Good Life Project

Harry Potter and the Sacred Text

Hidden Brain

Invisibilia

Magic Lessons with Elizabeth Gilbert

The Minimalists Podcast

Myths and Legends Podcast

On Being

The Robcast

Why Shamanism Now

Newsletters

Brain Pickings (www.brainpickings.org)

James Clear (www.jamesclear.com)

INDEX

Acorn, 177

Bell, 164

Blessing, 87, 152, 168, 178–180, 185–195, 197–199, 201, 204, 205

Blueing, 174

Breath work, 52–54, 57, 58, 74, 75, 88, 123, 127, 133–135, 138, 141, 143, 144, 147, 152

Bubble of light, 64, 66, 143

Burning, 12, 42, 50, 52, 64, 168

Camphor blocks, 175

Candle, 50, 51, 166–168

Chakras, 49, 50, 67, 206

Chaos, 55, 74, 85, 127, 143

Clearing, 1, 3, 5, 7, 9, 11–13, 16, 21, 23–25, 27, 29, 31, 37–42, 44, 46–50, 52–57, 61, 63, 68, 72–75, 77, 82, 87, 94–98, 100, 101, 104, 105, 107, 112, 120, 121, 123, 127, 128, 133–135, 138–141, 143–149, 152, 158, 160, 161, 163–165, 169, 170, 174, 176, 187, 205, 206

Clutter, 94, 99, 158

Consumption, 76, 78, 80

Consumerism, 75, 81, 87, 143, 152

Containing, 5, 37, 48, 61, 63, 64, 72–74,
    87, 101, 140, 143, 144, 167, 177

Contemplation, 89, 90, 144

Cording, 65, 143

Crystals, 40, 48, 57, 74, 75, 167, 171

Curiosity, 16, 108, 119–123, 125,
    136, 175, 183, 184, 197

Cultivation, 5, 7, 9, 11, 13, 16, 21, 24, 25, 41, 44, 47,
    53–55, 57, 63, 72–75, 83, 84, 87, 89, 91, 127, 128,
    135, 140, 143, 144, 148, 149, 163, 168, 170, 182, 187

Dancing, 41, 42, 45, 46

Decording, 65–67, 152, 206

Discernment, 16, 71, 78, 104, 119,
    120, 122, 136, 153, 181, 191

Drum, 47

Emotional acceptance, 107, 108, 116, 121, 197

Emotional body, 28, 41, 46, 119

Emotional denial, 109, 110

Emotional indulgence, 111, 112, 137

Energy, 1–29, 31–35, 37–54, 56–61, 63–80, 82–90, 92–101, 107, 109, 111–113, 117, 119, 120, 122–125, 127–129, 131, 133, 135–147, 149, 150, 152–155, 157–195, 197, 205–206

Energy body, 14, 17–20, 22, 24–29, 32, 37, 39, 41–44, 50, 51, 54, 56, 60, 63–66, 69, 70, 72–74, 76–78, 80, 82, 87, 90, 92, 93, 107, 117, 119, 135, 138, 140, 144, 149, 153, 154, 160, 162, 178, 182, 188

Energetic harmony, 14, 21–26, 28, 29, 31–34, 44, 66, 71, 74, 96, 140, 144, 160, 161, 183, 186

Essential oils, 48, 69, 166, 173, 174

Florida water, 174, 175

Gratitude, 65, 74, 86, 87, 135, 144

Himalayan salt lamp, 12, 174, 175

Incense, 52, 53, 166, 168, 171, 176

Infused, 49, 166

Infusion, 48, 70

Journal, 7, 8, 31, 35, 42, 61, 115, 123, 127, 139, 140

Judgment, 16, 99, 104, 107, 119–123, 136, 153, 179, 181, 183

Justification, 119, 120, 122, 124–128, 130, 133, 136, 137, 149, 150

Lavender, 48, 69, 168, 171, 177

Media, 64, 76–78, 80, 121, 144, 193

Meditation, 41, 49, 51, 59, 89, 90, 113, 127, 148

Mental body, 27, 78, 119

Mountain pose, 42–44, 58, 66, 138, 141, 168

Nap, 58

Peppermint, 173, 174

Practice, 1, 3, 6–8, 10, 11, 14, 15, 17, 19, 31, 38–43, 45, 51, 52, 54–59, 61, 63, 64, 66, 68, 70, 71, 74, 79, 80, 86–90, 92, 93, 96, 105, 117, 122, 134, 135, 138–141, 144, 145, 149, 150, 152, 157, 162, 175, 180, 187, 188, 194, 205

Prayer, 59, 68, 89, 90, 144, 148, 152, 186, 205

Principle of correspondence, 17, 29, 37, 87

Rattle, 47, 165, 168, 169

Reaction, 1, 22, 77, 105, 115, 122, 148, 149, 153

Reckitt's Crown Blue Squares, 174

Reflection, 67, 78, 89, 91, 113, 146, 152

Reproach, 119, 120, 122, 130–137, 149

Response, 15, 105, 112, 130, 149, 186

Rose quartz, 75, 177

Rose water, 168

Runes, 167, 168, 171, 176, 177

Sage, 12, 42, 48, 49, 52, 53, 94, 158, 166, 167, 169, 171

Salt, 12, 48, 57, 69, 167, 168, 171, 174–177

Shadow, 20, 97–101, 105, 107, 111, 114, 119,
    137, 138, 145, 146, 148, 162, 179, 184

Shadow closet, 98–101, 107, 111, 114,
    119, 137, 138, 145, 146, 148

Skin, 19, 20, 48, 63, 64, 69, 70, 161, 162

Sleep, 24–26, 32, 37, 87, 131, 174, 193

Smudging, 52, 53

Stones, 75, 167, 168, 171

Thieves oil, 174

Thoughtform, 27, 28, 78

Tiger's-eye, 57, 206

Trees, 4, 57, 133, 188

Triggers, 22, 92, 96, 101, 104, 120, 145

Values, 11, 12, 25, 33–35, 37, 60, 70–72, 76, 78, 80–82,
    84, 90, 95–97, 99, 100, 105, 112, 113, 116, 121, 124,
    125, 127–129, 136, 138, 147, 153, 155, 157, 161,
    162, 168, 170, 179, 183–185, 188, 193, 195, 197

Visualization, 47, 50, 88, 206

Water, 47–51, 70, 129, 166–168, 171–175, 191, 206

Water fountain, 172, 175

Wind chimes, 172

Wounds, 22, 83, 92, 95–97, 101, 104,
    119, 130, 133, 145, 181

Yoga, 42, 43, 46, 68, 86, 89, 140, 143, 152

GET MORE AT LLEWELLYN.COM

Visit us online to browse hundreds of our books and decks, plus sign up to receive our e-newsletters and exclusive online offers.

- **Free tarot readings • Spell-a-Day • Moon phases**
- **Recipes, spells, and tips • Blogs • Encyclopedia**
- **Author interviews, articles, and upcoming events**

GET SOCIAL WITH LLEWELLYN

Find us on   @LlewellynBooks

www.Facebook.com/LlewellynBooks

GET BOOKS AT LLEWELLYN

LLEWELLYN ORDERING INFORMATION

Order online: Visit our website at www.llewellyn.com to select your books and place an order on our secure server.

Order by phone:
- Call toll free within the US at 1-877-NEW-WRLD (1-877-639-9753)
- We accept VISA, MasterCard, American Express, and Discover.

Order by mail:
Send the full price of your order (MN residents add 6.875% sales tax) in US funds plus postage and handling to: Llewellyn Worldwide, 2143 Wooddale Drive, Woodbury, MN 55125-2989

POSTAGE AND HANDLING

STANDARD (US):(Please allow 12 business days)
$30.00 and under, add $6.00.
$30.01 and over, FREE SHIPPING.

CANADA:
We cannot ship to Canada. Please shop your local bookstore or Amazon Canada.

INTERNATIONAL:
Customers pay the actual shipping cost to the final destination, which includes tracking information.

Visit us online for more shipping options.
Prices subject to change.

FREE CATALOG!

To order, call
1-877-
NEW-WRLD
ext. 8236
or visit our
website